Curtain Call

A Mother/Daughter Story of Triumph Over Adversity

Patti Fields

ISBN 0-7414-0815-5

Published by:

INFI∞ITY
PUBLISHING.COM

Infinity Publishing.com
519 West Lancaster Avenue
Haverford, PA 19041-1413
Info@buybooksontheweb.com
www.buybooksontheweb.com
Toll-free (877) BUY BOOK
Local Phone (610) 520-2500
Fax (610) 519-0261

Printed in the United States of America

Printed on Recycled Paper

Published November, 2001

For my grandsons,
Ben and Jack

"I believe the life of a soul on earth lasts beyond its departure. I will always feel her life touching me...her voice speaking to me...her spirit in all the familiar things she touched, worked with and loved. She lives on in my life and the lives of all the others who knew and loved her."

Author unknown

CONTENTS

ACKNOWLEDGEMENTS

My purpose for writing this book was to continue the work of my daughter, Dee Dee. This truly was a collaborative effort and I am deeply grateful for each of the special people who shared their lives with Dee Dee and helped me bring this project to fruition. Thank you for being special lights—Kelly Etter Beilfus, Patrick Gendusa, Dr. Lonnie Kliever, Robert Krolik, Al McKittrick, Marney Makridakis, Dr. Donna Northouse, Cara Robinson, Jennifer Roth and Melanie Shapiro.

Thank you Marlene Renee for leading me to Tom Bird's seminar, and thank you Tom Bird for giving me a pathway to this book.

To each and every one of you who labored over the manuscript with me, I offer my sincere thanks for your time and patience. To my extraordinary editorial "staff" thank you: Paul Weisberg, Susan Shapiro, Dr. Wendy Harpham, and Pat O'Connell. I also want to thank Al McKittrick, Ernie Shapiro and Steven Young for their critical input.

I do not have enough ways to say thank you to every person who has believed in and encouraged me, especially my mother, Minnie Gassner (of blessed memory), my father, Irving Gassner, my son, Alan and his wife, Denise, and my special cheerleaders, Nancy Hodgson, Dr. Alexandra Levine, Arlene Fieldsteel, Arlene Weisberg and Patrick Gendusa.

A special thanks goes to my wonderful husband, Howard, for his enduring love, support and encouragement.

INTRODUCTION

You might say that this is the story of a nice, young, Jewish heterosexual woman from a good home who died from AIDS. So what is different or new here? Lots of people, even nice young women, have died from complications from AIDS. Why was Dee Dee's experience any different?

Dee Dee's instantaneous response to her affliction was special and unique. As it says in the Talmud, "If you save one life, you save the world." Dee Dee quickly developed a fierce determination to save the lives of other young adults, especially women, and to educate them about the risk of a disease that in 1993-1995 was definitely a gay white male disease in the eyes of the American public.

Dee Dee's battle during the last nine months of her life was one of constant loss of physical abilities. She met the progressive deterioration with a calmness and maturity far beyond her years. She may have entered adulthood with much trepidation but her departure from it was one of grace and poise.

This is a true story of an ever-so-human mother caught between many rocks and more hard places. And it is a tale of one tiny courageous young woman and her response to a life-threatening illness.

Dee Dee especially wanted to reach young sexually active women so that some day they would not have to look in retrospect at what they might have done differently. In that spirit this could be viewed as a coming-of-age gift book, but it is really for anyone of *any* age who is sexually active.

From this story, Dee Dee and I hope that you will stop and think twice before acting in some manner to put *your* life at risk. After you read it, you may want to share this book with someone in whose life it could make a difference. *Be safe*, for your life is our hope for a bright future.

The first anniversary—a time to remember and re-flect. I had celebrated many anniversaries over the years, but this one was different. Without a guidebook to point the way, I did not know how to commemorate the first anniversary of my daughter's death. I could not bear to be alone and did not want her husband to be alone either. My husband could not join me due to a pressing business commitment.

For Howard, a deeply religious man, the eleventh of Tammuz on the Hebrew calendar would forever be our day of remembrance of our daughter, Dee Dee. On that day, this year and every year, Howard and I would be together.

But for Dee Dee's husband, Al and for all of the other loved ones in her life, June 28 would be the anniversary of her passing.

Al greeted me at the airport with a lingering hug and eyes that betrayed his still-raw pain. Then we chatted as we always did on the drive to their home near downtown. Along the way, he told me about a new woman in his life. Al's new love felt like a betrayal even though I knew my daughter wanted him to go on living after she was gone. I was relieved to learn that his lady friend had plans to be out of town for the weekend.

As we parked in front of their little Victorian house, I recalled how proud my daughter had been the day they had purchased it just a few years ago. On the surface it appeared the same as it did before. Yet everything had changed.

Inside the door, Patch, the Jack Russell terrier I adored, greeted me warmly. Al carried my suitcase upstairs and left me alone to give me some time for my thoughts and feelings to settle. It was in this house that so much joy had been shared. And it was here that I had said goodbye to my daughter, my baby girl.

After unpacking I joined Al in the living room to play the photomontage video of Dee Dee's life that I had produced back home in Dallas. A videographer-friend had helped me sequence photographs of her, beginning with her childhood and continuing until her infection with HIV. I narrated the tribute, reading the story of Dee Dee's life as she had told it whenever she did an AIDS presentation. We added more photographs of her after she was infected with HIV and I read her diary entry, the one she wrote one week following her AIDS diagnosis. Then the screen faded to black and flashed her birth date—September 19, 1968—and the date of her death—June 28, 1996.

Twenty-seven years old.

The video ended with a clip of Dee Dee singing *Somewhere Over the Rainbow* at the first National Mothers March against AIDS in Washington, D.C, May '95. A ten-minute video captured her life—a life gone-too-soon.

Even though Al and I had lived the story, the documentary left us both spellbound. A silence hung in the air for several moments after static had filled the screen. It was a powerful story—a cautionary tale for all, and a glorious measure of one woman's life.

At exactly 9 p.m. on Saturday, June 28, Al and I lit a candle. We sat in what was once Dee Dee's room and allowed our own quiet memories of her to mingle with our tears. Then we went into the backyard and released one rosy-pink balloon into the night sky.

As we watched it drift away, the phone rang. Friends and family called and kept calling all night long. So many people touched by one petite, courageous woman. It was what we, the survivors, needed to know most of all—she lived on in the hearts and loving memories of others.

The following Tuesday, Al and I tucked Dee Dee's video into a canvas tote bag. We drove to Boulder for an AIDS 101 presentation that he had volunteered us both to give in a home for at-risk teenaged girls. The talk was sponsored by the Boulder Colorado AIDS Project. The night I had arrived in Denver Al had mentioned the BCAP presentation and I had many misgivings. I knew that I wanted to tell Dee Dee's story and had always felt comfortable with public speaking in other venues. But this time it was different. I was not sure I was ready.

The night before as I lay in bed, Dee Dee came to me for the first time since her death. I saw her effervescent smile and felt the pressure of an unseen hand on my shoulder. "Relax, Mom," she said. "You'll do fine."

Al paused on the steps outside the modest but tidy Boulder group-home to share a smoke with a couple of the teens. Shortly thereafter, one by one the girls sauntered into the sparsely furnished living room as each one completed her evening chores.

I had no illusion about our audience. These were street-wise girls—some gang members, some truants and runaways. Some had arrest records. For a few the next step could be prison. And I was sure that all of them were intimately familiar with sex and drugs.

"Where's the cute guy?" one of the girls whispered loudly to her friend and then nodded her head toward me. "What's *she* doing here? We usually get a gay guy to do this AIDS stuff."

This was perhaps their first clue that tonight's presentation would be unlike any they had heard before. I closed my eyes for a minute and could see and hear my daughter as she sounded the first time I attended one of her presentations. I recalled the almost imperceptible gasp that had escaped from the audience when she made her opening statement.

Simply and in a forthright manner she would say, "Hi. I'm Dee Dee Fields-McKittrick. I'm 25 years old. I'm married. And, I'm a woman living...with...AIDS." Like a lightbulb crashing on a ceramic tile floor, Dee Dee shattered every stereotype anyone might have had about AIDS.

I asked myself, "What could I, the mother of a daughter who died from AIDS, possibly say that would have that kind of impact?"

Then I thought about my world only six years ago when my daughter had graduated college full of hope. I recalled her as she had grown into an inspiring young woman—a student of musical theater in New York City and then a working actress touring the country—living her dream and falling in love.

And finally, in the face of nine street-hardened girls with their lives balanced so precariously on the edge, I remembered how easily and quickly our world in one moment had changed forever. I knew exactly what I had to say.

Chapter One

GIFT-OF-TIME
June-July 1992

Dee Dee and I were both on the precipice of our new wonderful lives. I had finally reached that stage in a mother's life when, at last, I could exhale. Both of my children were grown. They were living their own lives. Howard and I had raised our son and daughter in Dallas, Texas. I always said that if our son got his wish, he would be living on a mountaintop in Colorado and if our daughter got her heart's desire, she would be living in the middle of Manhattan. Alan, at age 26, was married and living on that mountaintop in Colorado. And Dee Dee, at age 23, was living on the upper West Side of Manhattan, studying musical theater at the American Academy of Dramatic Arts. Life was perfect.

Howard and I were doing our usual Saturday morning errands when he turned to me and said, "Patti, what do you *really* want for your 50th birthday?"

Knowing Howard the way that I do, I had anticipated his question and I had already given much thought to my answer. "I don't want jewelry or anything of monetary value. I want a gift of *time*—one year off work. Time just for me to do whatever I want to do, whenever I want to do it!"

I am not sure my sweet husband understood it. I am not even sure that I did. I just knew that I had this need. Howard, being the loving supportive man he had been for thirty years of marriage, said, "Sure. But could you keep a part-time involvement in our business? Could you continue to do our payroll and track my commissions at home? And would you still do some of our convention work with me?"

"You've got a deal," I told him. Howard silently decided to start his gift giving by throwing me not one but two surprise birthday parties. The first party was in Dallas at the end of June with our friends. Party number two was in Colorado on my actual birthday, July 3, with family and a few more close friends.

June 5, 1992

Daddy called this morning. He asked me to come to Colorado for a surprise party he was planning for Mom. He wanted me to be part of the surprise. "How fun," I thought. But I explained to him that I didn't know if I could get excused from my rehearsals for senior showcase. There was just no excuse for missing a rehearsal in the theater world short of death—my own. I really wanted to go to Mom's party. I decided to beg Richard, my pianist/director to let me go. I pulled what mom called my "Sarah Heartburn" act on him.

After Dad's call, I went to look for Richard. "You know me, Richard, I always meet my commitments. I wouldn't ask but this is such a special birthday for my mom. I've missed so many family events. Could I pleeease, pretty please, go? Whatdya think?"

Richard was so nice and understanding. I couldn't believe it. He excused me from two rehearsals so I could make the trip. I gave him a big hug. He was such a sweetie. Now all I needed was the perfect birthday present for Mom, but what would that be?

The next day I was pouring over old musical scores from obscure Broadway shows in the Lincoln Center Library. That's when it hit me. Why don't I find a special song and sing it to her? I'll bet I can get someone at school to make a piano track on an audiocassette for me. Now, all I need is the perfect song. Eureka!

Amazingly, I didn't have the slightest suspicion about either birthday party. The biggest surprise of all was seeing Dee Dee in Colorado. When she told me that she had to get excused from rehearsals to come to my birthday party, I knew two things: this was a very special birthday, and my daughter knew how to use her talent to move others.

Dee Dee gathered everyone around her and filled our friends' home and my heart with her special gift: song. There was not a dry eye in the house after she sang *Mama, A Rainbow* from the show *Minnie's Boys*. The words lose something when read instead of heard in her belting soprano voice, but I wanted to share those haunting lyrics with you. Somehow my daughter knew intuitively that at age 50 I was beginning to feel old.

Mama A Rainbow
by
Hal Hackady and Larry Grossman

What do you give, to the lady who has given all her life and love to you?
What do you give, to the reason you are living?
I could window-shop the world before I'm through.

Mama, a rainbow...Mama a sunrise...Mama the moon to wear...That's not good enough...no not good enough...Not for Mama.

Mama, a palace...Diamonds like doorknobs, Mountains of gold to spare...That's not rich enough...no not rich enough...Not for Mama.
Mama a lifetime...crowded with laughter...That's not long enough...not half long enough...

What can I give you? That I can give you. What will your present be?

Mama...young and beautiful...always young and beautiful That's the Mama...I'll always see...
That's for Mama with love from me.

Chapter Two

CINDERELLA TOUR
Summer 1993

July 6, 1992

I had a great time at Mom's birthday party. I didn't get home until after midnight last night. The airport was a zoo and the taxi to the apartment a nightmare. So what else is new in this city?

I better get myself ready for rehearsal tonight. Senior showcase is only a few weeks away. The straight acting bit will be easy for me. I just about know all my lines. My song needs a little more work. But the dance routines—ugh! I dread them. Maybe I can get Kelly to help me with them.

I can't believe that I have almost completed my 15-month program at AMDA. It's kind of scary and exciting. I'm reading every issue of Backstage *for theater auditions. It's funny. When I accepted the invitation to attend AMDA last year I was about to graduate from St. Edward's University in Austin, Texas. So I knew the rule about no auditioning from AMDA but I didn't care. After all, I was lucky to have done a number of shows at St. Ed's. And even though I hated the experience, I did do summer stock in Granbury, Texas.*

I had to laugh when I thought of the delay because it reminded me of my first year in college at the University of Miami. Mom said that I suffered stage withdrawal at that time. True, before I went to Miami, I had done a lot of theater performances in Dallas so I missed being on a stage. I have to admit I was pretty darn miserable in Miami during my freshman year because the school didn't allow any audition- ing either. This time it's different. The people at AMDA cast me in their last senior showcase. They don't care if I sing in the cabaret clubs in the Village either. They just don't want me to do any theater gigs.

My favorite club in the Village is the Duplex. My roomies and I regularly hang out there. I love singing on their open mike nights. One night I boldly entered a "Stars of Tomorrow" contest, and I won! My prize was a one-night booking for a 45-minute cabaret show on a mid-week night at the club. Boy, am I thrilled! Since I need to provide my own accompanist, I'm lucky that I have just helped "Marie"(not her real name), my best friend, move to New York. She plays piano well and her alto blends beautifully with my mezzo- soprano voice. We did a lot of performing together in high school. So what if we only have ten days to throw a show together? We can do it!

Dee Dee called to invite me to her cabaret show. She was so happy. Her high-pitched voice and rapid-fired speech said it all.

"Mommy, Marie and I have a date to do a cabaret show at the Duplex. Can you and Daddy come?"

"Sure, honey, when is it?"

It really did not matter to me. She did not have to ask me twice to come to New York. I had promised myself early in my daughter's career to go to as many of her performances as I could. Over the years, I had sat in some pretty offbeat theater spaces and witnessed a varying quality of shows, but I would not trade anything for those times and memories.

The Duplex was located in the heart of the Village. Howard and I climbed the flight of steps to the bar. Next to the bar was this small rectangular clubroom. It reminded me of the coffeehouses in the '50s. The walls were black. The room was filled with small tables. In the center of each table was a dimly lit candlelight lamp. The simple, naked stage was at the end of the room with a barstool and a microphone. The piano was placed strategically to the left of the setup. Wanting to remain unobtrusive, I stood in the back of the room before the show began.

The owner of the club said to me, "I've seen a lot of these kids come and go. That one," she said pointing to my daughter, "has what it takes to make it to Broadway. That is, if she stays well."

I was very flattered by the compliment, especially since the owner had no idea that I was Dee Dee's mom, but what did she mean by "if she stays well," I thought. She had been sickly as a child but the owner did not know that. Maybe she was talking about the stress of the business or dealing with the irregular schedule. Or was it something else?

July 15, 1992

The summer has been unbelievably hectic. My life is such a whirlwind. The cabaret show with Marie was great fun. I loved finding little-known songs with great lyrics. Marie and I wove them together to tell the story of two old friends reuniting. Art imitating life! I'm so glad that Mom and Dad got to see the show. I know how much Mom worries about me. I just want her to be proud of me.

Marie and I were lucky to get a second booking at the Duplex for August. I guess they liked our show. We're re-working it. I think we need to do a little more patter and Marie has a few different songs she'd like us to try. We've been friends since the day we met at Arts. I was 18 and she was 15. Mom even thinks of her as a second daughter. We are all so close. Back then Marie and I had a dream of someday living in an apartment in New York while we pursued our theater careers. It's hard to believe that we are living our dream. I don't think either of us has stopped to enjoy these moments because so much is happening in both of our lives.

In addition to the cabaret act, I still have classes from AMDA, rehearsals for senior showcase, and my job teaching gymnastics to the little kids at Circus Gymnastics. I

*must make an appointment to get my head shot photos taken
and I have to prepare my résumé. It's a no wonder that I'm
so tired all the time.*

I always marveled at everything Dee Dee would take
upon her little shoulders. At barely five feet tall and maybe
ninety-five pounds on a good day, her boundless energy reminded me of the Energizer bunny. From our numerous telephone conversations, I could tell from the sound of her voice
that she was happy with her life in New York even with all
its pressures and demands. She had the right temperament
and energy for the pace in New York and loved "The City."

Toward the end of that summer, I started my gift of
time. The first thing on my list was an audition for member-
ship in the Contemporary Chorale, an all-woman, vocal and
dance performance group. Being an amateur singer and a
marginal dancer, I was thrilled to be accepted. A few weeks
later, I enrolled in a writing course and a computer class at
one of our local colleges. It was a special joy just to recon-
nect with women friends and exercise regularly and consis-
tently at my club. It was a pleasure to simply be able to read
books from cover to cover without interruption or play bridge
when I felt so motivated. It was a deliciously fun time.

I wanted to do some hands-on charitable work, but I
was not sure what that would be. Volunteer work was a big
part of my life when my children were small. I had to let that
go when I returned to work, but I continued to support my
favorite charities financially. My birthday present gave me
time to give, but I had not decided yet to whom.

August 1, 1992
*The purpose of senior showcase is to help us find
theatrical agents. My personal observation: only a few
agents come to the AMDA showcases. I've only seen a
handful of students sign with agents when they graduate. So I
better "go for it" on my own.*

I'm continuing to read the pages of Backstage. I also check the Equity Callboard on 44 Street, too. I am there almost every day. I jot down anything that might seem right for me. I do not want to do any "cattle calls." If the audition says "by appointment," I will call.

I know I am best suited for children's theater productions. I have "the look"—a small body, a youthful face, and loads of energy. It also helps that I've done so much children's theater—Peter Pan; The Lion, The Witch and The Wardrobe; Prodigy; and Tales of a Fourth Grade Nothing at Dallas Children's Theater. I even did a production of Cinderella for the Dallas Theater Center when I was sixteen. But the best part of my résumé has to be my six-week tour of the Soviet Union in Peace Child.

There's a production of Heidi holding auditions by appointment next week. I'm going to call for a time. I've learned from my Daddy how to sell myself, so this should be easy. It's a good thing that I took the audition workshops offered by AMDA. I know I have to bring my head shot with my résumé attached to the back of it. I've prepared a song and a monologue. I know that I'll only get to sing sixteen bars of the song; directors can tell from those few measures of music if I have what it takes.

Hopefully I won't have to do a "cold reading." Just in case, I'll read Heidi after my appointment is made. I like to get that first read under my belt. Then if I am asked to read something from the script, it won't quite feel like a cold reading. Learning disabilities make cold readings a big challenge for me. Anyhow, it's fun to look through the story for all the roles a character actress like me can play. The ingenue roles belong to the beautiful blond divas. Then there's me, a Fanny Brice look alike.

Ten years of auditioning in high school, Dallas theaters, colleges and my fair share of rejection have taught me one thing: even if I have a terrific audition, the director still might not cast me in his show simply because I do not fit his vision for his particular production. Oh well, that's the life of an actor!

August 20, 1992

This morning I did my first New York professional theater auditions! Wow. I had no trouble finding the Loft *audition space on 42 street. When I stepped onto that huge empty stage, I felt wiggy, a strange mix of emotions— excited, nervous and scared all wrapped together. The audition went very fast. I felt that I did well, but who knows? No matter. I went to do my next audition for a production of* Cinderella.

It was a very full day. When I returned to the apartment, I was beat. Marie and Kelly asked me how the auditions went. I told them I thought I did okay. Still, I don't think anyone was more shocked than I was when I got callbacks from both auditions! The first thing I did after my roomies peeled me down from the ceiling was to call Mom.

"Mommy, I got callbacks from both auditions! Which show do you think I should take if I get offers from both of them?"

Both of the shows were road tours. *Heidi* was a three-month tour and *Cinderella* was a nine-month tour. "Do you know anything about either of the production companies?" I queried her knowing full well that she probably had not researched either one. I could tell that she was leaning toward the nine-month tour, if she could get it. "Don't you think that nine months on the road will be too rough?"

"No, Mom. And besides, just think how great a nine-month tour will look on my résumé."

"I don't know, Dee Dee," I said voicing my doubts.
A few days later Dee Dee called. "I got cast as one of the evil stepsisters, Henrietta, in *Cinderella*, Mom. I'm taking it!"

No need for any further discussion. My daughter was ecstatic. "Earth to Dee Dee." I tried *not* to deflate her bubble, but there were so many practical matters for her to consider and that was the role I played, practical Mom. Rehearsals for the tour started in Denver on September 1. I rambled off a host of my concerns.

"What about AMDA? Will they graduate you in mid-September even though you cannot quite complete their program? Can you sublet your apartment? Can you get one of your roommates to take over your role of collecting and paying the rent? What about your job?"

"Oh, Mom," she groaned.

One by one, Dee Dee buttoned down the pieces of her life in New York as she prepared to leave the City. She had to scramble to leave for tour on such short notice. She easily found someone to take her place in her apartment. Places to live in New York were always at a premium, and sharing the rent with three other actresses made this apartment on the upper West Side of Manhattan very attractive. Well, to another starving actress, that is. So, I was not surprised that she was able to do this quickly.

She then asked Marie, who had just been added to the group of roommates, to collect and pay the rent. She was glad that Marie agreed to do it. She was definitely the most responsible one of the group. Marie acted happy for her friend's good fortune but underneath she felt sad. Once again she would be separated from her best friend.

Dee Dee then spoke to her AMDA counselor about graduation. He said he was so proud of her winning a role in *Cinderella.* Since the goal of the school was to help their students find work, he felt certain he could arrange for her to get her certificate of completion in mid-September, even though she would leave the program a few weeks before it officially ended to prepare for her tour.

Dee Dee gave notice at Circus Gymnastics where she had worked since she had arrived in New York. The owner was happy for Dee Dee but she, too, worried about replacing her. Not only was Dee Dee an instructor, but she also organized and directed the birthday parties sponsored by the gym. She even had a key to the place and often found new teachers for them from among her friends. Dee Dee promised to call the owner the minute she returned to New York. She was told that there would always be a position

14

available for her at Circus Gymnastics. When Dee Dee told me this, I felt so proud of her.

All that remained, besides packing up and shipping some of her stuff home, was for Dee Dee to do her senior showcase. Howard and I were fortunate to return to New York at the end of August to catch the show. In addition to an acting scene, Dee Dee sang *On My Own* from *Les Misérables.* At first I was puzzled by the selection of that song. Dee Dee usually belted a song or sang comedic, cutesy upbeat numbers befitting her appearance. This song was dramatic and mature. To my surprise, Dee Dee delivered. The song spoke volumes—the lyrics most prophetic. The small New York audience gave her a standing ovation.

Unfortunately, Dee Dee did not sign with a theatrical agent. It did not matter to her because she already had a job. She would be a *working* actress and that was the apex to her. In a few short days she would be in rehearsals for *Cinderella* in Denver, Colorado—her first professional national tour.

Chapter Three

ONE OF THE EVIL (NOT UGLY) STEPSISTERS
September 1992-April 1993

September 2, 1992

I arrived in Denver yesterday. I feel like Alice in Wonderland falling down that hole. Oops! Here I am, but what am I doing here? I've had lots of practice at dropping myself into strange situations. I did it when I enrolled in the Arts Magnet High School in Dallas and the University of Miami and when I left the country to do Peace Child *in the Soviet Union. Surely I knew no one at St. Edward's University or even AMDA before I moved to New York. All that doesn't help. I'm scared.*

Mom says that I never knew a stranger. She thinks that I can talk to a brick wall and get a response. I feel that I don't fit in until I get to know everyone I am with. I hate to admit it, but transitions in my life have always been this difficult. I wonder why that is.

Mom wasn't surprised when my first calls home were a bunch of complaints. Boy, did I grouse. I didn't like my roommate. I didn't care much for the other kids in the cast. What a bunch of immature, egotistical actors! What did I expect? Mom just listened.

I wrote Marie that this was not how I visualized my life after AMDA. I thought that I would be living the life of a starving actress going from audition to audition, working for Circus Gymnastics just to pay the rent, and maybe finally having some time for a serious boyfriend. How did I wind up in Denver with THESE people?

Marie called and set me straight. She reminded me that I was SO lucky to be a working actress. "Remember Miss Smith giving us THE TALK on our first day at Arts?"

"Yeah," I lamely replied.

"Ninety-eight percent of all actors are unemployed... blah, blah. And we vowed we would be in that two percent?" Marie prodded.

"Yeah...but..."

"No buts, Dee Dee. Stop your whining. Remember, you are very blessed."

After our conversation I realized that Marie was right and perhaps I needed an attitude adjustment. So, after rehearsal the next evening, I joined some of the cast and went with them to one of the local clubs. Our music director, Al, was at the club. He was easy to spot in the crowd. His thick wavy blond hair was a big giveaway. He was with some woman who was not in our production company. I figured she was his girlfriend. "Great, the cutest guy in our company has a girlfriend. This is going to be a very long trip. Guess I am just going to have to learn my lines and songs and write in my journal."

The role of Henrietta, one of the evil (not ugly) stepsisters, came easy to me. I memorized my lines quickly and was one of the first people in the cast to be off script. From a young age memorizing was how I learned. My reading tutor called it one of the compensation skills of having learning disabilities. We had just three weeks to get the show up which was typical for a professional theatrical production.

September 10, 1992

I wasn't being antisocial but I wasn't into the club scene either. I had been there and done that in college. So, after rehearsals I went back to my room and watched TV or read or wrote a diary entry. Last night Al and I were work-

ing some of the numbers from the show kinda late when he said, "Let's grab a bite to eat when we finish here."

"Sure," I smiled.

That evening he told me he wasn't much into socializing with the cast either. He said that he didn't like to drink like us kids do.

"EXCUSE ME?" I said emphatically, my hazel eyes going black like they always did when I got miffed.

"Kids? How old are you?" I asked him.

"Forty-two."

"Well, I never would have guessed. You look and act about 10 years younger."

He laughed. "Guess, then, we're even," he said with a sheepish grin. I asked him about the woman he was with the other evening.

"Oh, her, the diva? She and I are finished."

It was a pleasant evening. Al was a nice guy. At least I found someone I could talk to. In a couple of weeks the tour will open in Colorado Springs and then we go to Hays, Kansas. All the "high" spots in the world, huh?

Dee Dee stopped complaining to me shortly after the tour began. I figured it was her typical pattern. After another rough transition, she had finally adjusted to her new surroundings. Little did I know that she had begun a relationship with the music director. I was happy if she was happy, and she did sound a lot happier.

Shortly thereafter, I began to hear about this guy, Al, from Dee Dee almost every time we spoke.

October 15, 1992

We really became a couple in Hays, Kansas after that one evening. When we arrived, Al asked me if I'd like to do dinner with him. We had just spent four hours chatting on the drive from Denver to Hays. I think I surprised Al with my vast knowledge of musical theatre and I felt he was somewhat intrigued with me.

"Sure. I'd love to do dinner. Where?"

Al suggested a nearby International House of Pancakes. At dinner, we talked about living in the West. I told him about growing up in Dallas and moving to New York to go to AMDA and how I missed the open spaces and seeing the stars at night.

"We are in western Kansas. Probably right outside of town we could see millions of stars."

Later Al swore to me that his intent was to just show me the stars...that he felt like a big brother. When we borrowed the van, Michael, our tour manager, looked over his glasses at Al and gave him a look that said, "What are you trying to pull here?"

We took a ride into the countryside and parked. We got out of the van and watched the sun set. Then we watched the stars appear in the sky to the west. We talked for hours about everything—the cast, the show, theater, our careers, our past relationships, HIV, our life goals, etc. At the end of the evening we kissed and then we kissed again. Al was gentle and sweet.

He placed his finger under my chin and tipped my face to his and said, "Where have you been all my life?"

I smiled and said, "Growing up!"

He laughed. I wasn't trying to be funny or cute. After all, there was an 18-year difference in our ages.

Within days we were falling very quickly in love and we soon became inseparable. Within a few weeks, I moved into Al's single room. It would have been a glorious tour if it weren't for two things: the members of the cast teased us all the time, and I kept getting sick.

After Kansas, the tour was scheduled to play St. Charles, Illinois. Dee Dee's grandparents, who lived nearby in Chicago, went to see the show. They said they loved it. Probably they loved seeing their granddaughter on stage more than anything else. After the show, Dee Dee introduced them to Al. "Grandma Minnie and Grandpa Irving, I want you to meet Al. He's our music director," she told them without mentioning his status as her new boyfriend.

October 30, 1992

The bad news: As the tour rolls from town to town, I make whoever is driving the van (we take turns) stop at a doc-in-the box emergency clinic along the way. I had a cold last week and got a prescription for an antibiotic. After I took it, I felt better for a little while, and now I feel sick again. I am accustomed to not feeling well because as a kid I always felt lousy. To add to my frustration, the manager of the tour is either late with our paychecks or our paychecks bounce.

The good news: I'm beginning to like some of the cast members. Annie, our fairy Godmother, is just the nicest person. So is Steve. Poor guy, he's a diabetic. He has been so sympathetic about my being sick. My special love is Darryl, the only black member of our cast. Darryl with his drums and Al with his synthesizer are our "orchestra." Musicians are different from actors! If it weren't for Al, and those few others, I know I would have given serious consideration to resigning the tour after my minimum three-month obligation. Steve says that he plans to leave the tour in December, but he has diabetes and can't stay on the road any more.

I've been tucking little notes of encouragement in different people's scores and scripts and in Darryl's drum cases, just like the notes Mom used to leave in my lunch sacks when I was a little girl. It's my way of breaking the monotony of touring. Everyone is always surprised and pleased. I know whenever I found a little love note from Mom it always warmed me down to my toes.

Al and I have enjoyed walking the shores of the Atlantic in North Carolina and hiking the Smoky Mountains in Tennessee on our days off. I'm in love and for the first time, I feel comfortable with this man. He's romantic and caring and he even loves to cook and clean house!

Dee Dee found the touring life hard on her health and it worried me. The tour crisscrossed the country playing countless small towns for a day or two. Her environments

20

were constantly changing. There were many third-rate motels and dusty theater spaces, not to mention constant exposure to numerous kids. After all, *Cinderella* was a children's theater production and Dee Dee liked nothing better than to mingle with the kids following each show.

From birth, Dee Dee had been plagued with allergies, so when she called home from the tour to complain that she was sick, I was concerned but not particularly surprised given her life pattern. I could not understand why she didn't take better care of herself and felt a tide of frustration rising within me whenever she complained about being sick.

Dee Dee told me that she planned to come home over the Christmas holidays when the tour would go on hiatus. She asked me to make appointments for her with her doctors. She was looking forward to getting together with Marie in Dallas. Ever since Dee Dee and Marie became close friends, Dee Dee enjoyed Christmas mornings with Marie's family. The two girls planned to perform their cabaret show for our friends in our living room during their visit.

Reflecting on that Christmas, I remember how much I was looking forward to Dee Dee's visit and how disappointed I was that she was not interested in spending more time with me—or so it appeared. Sleep was high on her agenda and she did a lot of it. This did not surprise me either because that, too, was a typical Dee Dee pattern. Ever since she started her theater career at 14, she would push herself so hard. She would go 800 miles an hour and then collapse—typically when she returned home. Most people would describe Dee Dee as a kinetic ball of energy. To me, her Mom, I often saw the lightbulb after it burned out. So when Dee Dee returned from tour and slept all the time, I was annoyed but I was not particularly alarmed. At one point I suggested to her that perhaps the touring life was too hard on her. Would she consider resigning the tour? She would not hear of it. She would fulfill her nine-month commitment come hell or high water! She became angry and frustrated with me.

January 2, 1993

My visit home over the holidays was both wonderful and horrible. I enjoyed being off the road. It was great being in a real home with a bed and a kitchen to cook all my favorite vegetarian dishes. What was not so great was Mom. She became exasperated with all my sleeping. I know she was looking forward to my visit so we could do some mother/daughter things, but I was exhausted. All I wanted to do was sleep. When Mom suggested that I resign the tour, I just "blew." On top of all of this, I was missing Al. The two-week separation from him felt like it was never going to end.

Marie and I got into this terrible fight, too. First, it was because I didn't want to rehearse our cabaret show. She thought I didn't want to sing with her anymore. I loved singing with Marie. I was just too pooped to rehearse. We did our show and it went very well. Then we had our biggest fight ever. Marie suggested that I get tested for HIV. I thought she had a lot of nerve to even suggest that. Between the two of us, she was the promiscuous one, not me. We managed to part on good terms, thank goodness.

Dee Dee saw all of her doctors during that visit and no one picked up on anything wrong or different about her except for her dermatologist. He remarked that the series of bumps on her neck were viral growths (mollescum) and that it was an unusual condition for her to have. Her gynecologist reported a stage-two Pap smear. He said not to worry because he saw that all the time. He recommended that she get tested again when the tour ended in May. She complained to him about being plagued with chronic yeast infections, but her complaints did not raise any red flags for him either. Even our family internist, probably one of the best diagnosticians I have ever known, could not find anything seriously wrong with her. He knew something was not quite right, but it never occurred to him that it could be AIDS—not this cute, young, Jewish woman. He noted in his records, "could be allergies, weak constitution, etc." Having cared for her since she was a teenager, he expressed his frustration at never being able to get her 100 percent well. At that appointment, she told him that she did not want any more antibiotics. She asked him to refer her to a holistic doctor and he did.

By the time Dee Dee left Dallas, she was feeling much better. She was rested and looking forward to reuniting with Al at a bed-and-breakfast in Dayton, Ohio for a few days before the tour commenced.

January 10, 1993

I was happy when I returned to the tour. I felt so much better. I couldn't wait to see Al. I missed him terribly. I knew that I would return to the tour unless my doctors found something wrong with me. On the one hand, it was sort of a relief when they didn't find anything wrong. On the other hand, I was beginning to think this was all in my head. It was more than just feeling tired or having constant sinus and yeast infections. Why did I wake up soaked with perspiration? Why was my stomach always upset? I vowed that this would be the last time I would ever accept a nine-month tour. I obviously did not have the constitution for the touring life. Secretly, I knew Mom was right, but I never admitted it. In my mind, "the show must go on...."

After Dee Dee left town, I resumed my writing and singing. I was enjoying my gift of time. Even though my daughter was having her health challenges, she and my son seemed happy, successful and living their dreams. It could not get any better than that—or could it?

A couple of weeks later, my husband and I received a package in the mail from our son and his wife. Howard was on a business trip, so I just ripped open the box. I nearly flipped with excitement. In it was a photo album with an inscription that read: "For Grandma and Grandpa."My heart burst with happiness. Joy and goose bumps flooded my body when I learned that I was going to become "Grandma"!

January 13, 1993

It's funny. I felt fine when I returned to tour and shortly thereafter Al got sick with what we think was the flu. He ran a high fever, was exhausted, had a bronchial infection, a rash from head to foot, and oral ulceration. Fortunately, all this passed and he recovered within about a week.

A few weeks later, I was sick again with another sinus infection. "Oh, God," I thought. "What is the deal here?" I don't know how I made it through every show, but I never missed a performance. There were times when I worked for thirty or forty days straight without a day off. Sometimes I slept on the floor backstage during the intermission or between acts. But I was always "on" when I needed to be. After all...the show must go on. This had been imbedded in my brain ever since I began my training at Arts. Al expressed his concern about my health to me time and again.

The tour is going to play in Tyler, Texas in a couple of weeks. I know that Mom and Dad will make the drive from Dallas to see the show. I'll bet they can't wait to meet Al. I don't know why he had to write them that letter telling them all about his previous marriages and life. As my cousin said, he doesn't have the best résumé. I know he can charm Mom, but Dad is another story. God, I love Al. I hope the folks will, too.

The minute I met Al, I could see why Dee Dee was attracted to him. His Irish good looks hid his age and charm dripped from every pore. After the show, we took them both to dinner. Dee Dee was uncharacteristically very quiet. After dinner we drove them back to their hotel. Al asked us to wait in the lobby while he walked Dee Dee to their room. "A real gentleman," I thought.

When Al returned to the lobby, we sat and talked. He expressed his concern about Dee Dee's poor health, and said that he wondered if maybe she had mononucleosis. I told him that I did not think so because our internist had just thoroughly examined her, which included blood work. I also explained that none of her other doctors could find anything wrong with her either. While I was just as concerned as he was, I told him I thought we just had to conclude that the stress of road travel coupled with her allergies, sensitive system and eating mostly at fast food restaurants were just too much for her. I gave Al our residential 800-telephone number and urged him to keep in close contact with us. I told him that while Dee Dee might be a mature young lady to him, she could also be a stubborn little girl. We both agreed that she probably should not be doing such a long road tour.

It was April when I received the call. Al was on the line and said, "Your daughter wants to talk to you."

The phone transferred to Dee Dee. "Mommy, I'm re-signing the tour. Please send me a ticket home." She was crying and handed the phone back to Al.

"Dee Dee is okay. We're in the emergency room of a hospital in Lima, Ohio. She had an allergic reaction to a sul-fur-based antibiotic and we rushed her here. I really think she's okay." Al repeated, hastening to reassure us in an effort to lower our anxiety. "She's just very frightened."

I knew Dee Dee had to be very frightened and sick for her to make the gut-wrenching decision to resign the tour, but nothing could have prepared me for what I saw when she stepped off the airplane in Dallas a few days later. My daughter rarely wore makeup and had thin, pasty skin. But that day she was so pale that she looked as if every red blood cell had been drained out of her. Howard and I whisked her home and put her to bed. I called our family doctor and he agreed to see her the very next morning.

She awoke feeling a little better and said that she wanted to see the doctor by herself. I desperately wanted to go with her, but she was 24 years old and I had to accept the fact that she was an adult. As she left for her appointment she flippantly said to me, "I'm going to have Dr. Ted (not his real name) run every test on me including an HIV test."

I remember thinking, "Isn't that silly?" I told Howard what Dee Dee had said. He had grave concern but did not share it with me. Naively, I only gave it a few passing thoughts during the rest of that week. It just seemed like such a far-fetched scenario.

On Friday, Dee Dee was "vegging out" on the couch in our den when the phone rang. I answered it in the kitchen.

"Hi, Patti. This is Ted. Is Dee Dee there?" our doctor asked.

"Yes. I'll go get her."

"Patti, stay on the phone. I have something to say that I think both of you need to hear." So I told Dee Dee to pick up the phone in the den.

"Dee Dee, I have something to tell you," he began. "You asked me to call you as soon as I got the results. I ran both tests, the ELISA and the Western Blot, which is why it has taken me this long to get back to you." He hesitated and then lowered his voice to almost a whisper. "I am so sorry, but you are HIV positive."

Dee Dee threw down the phone and got hysterical. I ran to her. She was devastated.

It was April 9, 1993: 4 p.m.—a date and time that will burn in my heart forever.

Chapter Four

A STRANGE NEW WORLD
April 1993

*April 16, 1993 (*One week following Dee Dee's diagnosis)
How does someone of 24 begin to face the reality of AIDS and continue on? My life changed for me a week ago and now I have to meet the challenge or just give up. I am so scared but I know that in time, these feelings can and will turn to the courage I need to fight this illness.

So you listen to me VIRUS! I have lots of things left to do here. I am not ready to accept this death sentence. I want to live. I obviously have something to say and to do so that others someday won't have to fight you. I want you to hear me very clearly. I will and can stay healthy for as long as I need to. Thank you God for answered prayers. I am very thankful for the loved ones in my life, for all of their care and support.

This little light of mine, I'm gonna let it shine and shine and shine!

The shock from our doctor's stunning phone call numbed my entire body. I went on some kind of automatic mother-pilot that guided me to Dee Dee's side. She was crying hysterically and was absolutely inconsolable. I told myself to hold it together. Like the eye in a hurricane, I needed to remain calm for my daughter. I reached out to hold her.

"Don't touch me," she wailed. "Mommy, I don't want to die…not this way."

Her rejection of my affection puzzled me. I could not understand why she would not let me hold her.

"I know…I know…honey." I searched for what to say to my daughter.

I grabbed the phone and stupidly called Howard, who was in the car on his way home from work. I just blurted out, "Dee Dee is HIV positive!" It is a miracle that he did not wrap the car around a telephone pole while racing home to be with both of us.

Howard arrived home shortly thereafter and rushed to our daughter's side. "Dee Dee. You're not going to die, not today and not tomorrow," he said to her. Gradually, he soothed Dee Dee out of her hysteria. He was so good at that.

"Well, at least, Daddy, I know what's wrong with me," she sniffled.

Within an hour of receiving the news, my girlfriend just happened to call.

"Hello…" I could hardly get the words out of my mouth.

"What's the matter, Patti? You sound like something is terribly wrong."

"Ah….oh…it is." I hesitated again because I was not sure what to say. Then I just told her the truth. "Dee Dee is HIV positive!"

She offered to come right over to the house to comfort both of us. She was especially fond of Dee Dee, her kindred spirit.

"I don't think it's a good idea to come over just now."

She pressed on, "Then consider going somewhere with me tomorrow, anywhere. The three of you just can't sit in the house all weekend."

"We'll see. Call me tomorrow."

At first Dee Dee was annoyed at me for telling my girlfriend about her diagnosis. Then Dee Dee said, "I guess it's okay if she knows, but Mom, please, I don't want you to tell any more of your friends."

I understood. What was I thinking? She agreed that we needed to call her brother, Alan, and his wife, Denise, in Colorado to bring them into the loop.

"Alan, we have some terrible news…your sister is HIV positive." There was dead silence on the other end of the line. "Alan, are you there?"

"Yeah, Mom, I don't know what to say. Are you sure, I mean how do you know?"

I told him about the results from both tests. "Alan, what do you know about HIV?" I naively queried.

"I know plenty, Mom." He seemed to hesitate as he said something to Denise before continuing our conversation. "Denise's brother, Max, is HIV positive!"

"What?" I was dumbfounded and told Alan that I did not have a clue. We had been with him at numerous family gatherings. He looked so healthy and robust. I always thought of him as a Colorado mountain-man. He reminded me of Paul Bunyon, the tall lumberjack fictional character in his red flannel shirt, beard and tight blue jeans.

"Why didn't you tell me this before?"

"He's not public. Would you like him to call her?"

I learned one of my first lessons about HIV—not many people talk about it.

Later that evening, I told Dee Dee about Max and asked if she would speak to him if he called her. At first she said no but then she relented. Neither of us knew what we were saying or doing during those first hours. We had entered a strange new world and we felt like two lost aliens as we wandered around aimlessly.

Although Howard had calmed Dee Dee after Dr. Ted's phone call, she still would not let either of us hold or hug her. I felt rejected and confused but later I realized why she behaved that way. She thought she might be contagious, which became obvious when she grabbed up her tissues and paper bagged them.

"Don't touch those, Mom. I'll clean them up," she said as she grabbed her tissues and her juice glass. She put her glass into the dishwasher. It was out of character for her to clean up after herself.

During those early hours and days, I remember having twinges of fear dance through my head. Could I get infected from Dee Dee or the things she used? We both had so much to learn. Later, education taught us that people do not get infected from hugging or touching drinking glasses or tissues. I set aside my fears because my daughter needed me.

Dr. Ted called us later that evening and asked me why I hadn't called him.

"Oh, was I supposed to call you back?" I replied.

"I just thought you would have some questions for me. How are you and Dee Dee doing?" He was genuinely concerned about us.

I could not even form a question. Dr. Ted said he was leaving town for a few days and he wanted to give us his private telephone number at his vacation home. He requested the phone number of our pharmacy so he could order tranquilizers for Dee Dee and me. He then asked me if Howard was home because he wanted to speak with him.

Always the planner, Howard asked, "What's our next step?"

Dr. Ted said, "You need to see an infectious disease doctor who specializes in treating HIV."

"Could you get the names of those doctors for us?"

"Sure."

Dr. Ted called us back within a few minutes with the names of four doctors, one of whom was a woman. After a brief discussion with Dee Dee, we called Ted and asked him to set the appointment with the female HIV specialist.

April 11, 1993

I'm not sure what is worse—knowing that I'm HIV positive, telling Al and asking him to get tested, or seeing my parents deal with the devastating news. Mom and Dad are acting brave but I can see right through them. Their feelings are so transparent to me.

After I went ballistic with the news, I actually felt an odd sense of relief. Daddy quieted me down. I think the not-knowing-what-was-wrong-with-me for months was actually harder to bear than the news that I'm HIV positive. At least I finally know that something is wrong with me and that I'm not a mental case!

Yesterday, I called Al who was in Jackson, Wyoming (where the tour was) and Marie in New York and told them the bad news. Both of them were wonderful. They are making their plans to fly to Dallas to be with me. I won't make it through this without them. And, those dumb tranquilizers aren't helping much. Both Mom and me feel like two zombies. Mom says we should pitch the pills and I agree.

My girlfriend called back the next day and insisted all three of us go with her to a park. It was good to get out of the house and mix with other people. Dee Dee was most reluctant, but the outing lifted her spirits. The distraction was a good thing for all of us. Truthfully, the rest of that first weekend is nothing but a blur in my memory.

Timing is everything. I was about to start tech week with my chorale, which meant rehearsals every night with a band, sound checks and lighting checks for our big spring show. When I told Dee Dee that I was thinking about not doing the show, she shot me one of her looks and sternly said, "Mom, you WILL do the show! And, you WILL go to every rehearsal! I won't have this disease disrupt your whole life. Besides, the show must go on!"

Dee Dee was adamant but I was completely torn. On the one hand, I did not want to upset her any more than she already was and on the other hand, the last thing I wanted to do was sing and dance. Begrudgingly, I decided to do the show to relieve my daughter's guilt feelings.

The next day Dee Dee gave me a St. Genesius medal. "Mom, St. Genesius is the patron saint of all performers. I was given one by my teachers in high school to protect me when I was hanging lights on catwalks. The tradition says that you can't buy one. Another performer has to give it to you. I bought this for you while I was on tour after you told me that you joined the chorale. If you wear this medal when you perform, you'll always be protected and perform well."

I took it from her precious hands and wore it all tech week as well as during the show. (I wear it whenever I perform). Do not ask me how I did that show. I was running on "fumes." My strange new world felt cold and lonely. Not being allowed to tell anyone about my situation made things a thousand times more difficult for me. Though my daughter pressured me into doing the show against my wishes, in an odd way doing it was therapeutic. I learned another lesson about coping with HIV—keeping active and busy is helpful. "Busy-ness" forces the mind and the body to focus on something other than HIV at least for those moments and the distraction is a good thing.

April 12, 1993

On Monday, I saw my first infectious disease doctor, "Dr. Marianne"(not her real name). Mom came with me. From the moment the doctor and I met, I didn't like her. Her first comment to me was, "You don't look sick!" I thought, "That was a dumb thing to say. What was I supposed to look like—a tall gaunt, gay man?" Then she asked me to get on the scale. It surprised me that I weighed 100 pounds. My usual weight was 95 pounds. Guess all the touring, fast food and lying around the past few months have put a few pounds on me. I'm one of those people that rarely get on a scale. I've always been thin. In New York, I was in the best shape of my life, because I walked everywhere and worked out at Circus Gymnastics. For the past few months, my only exercise on tour was dancing in the show. We drove everywhere and I slept every chance I got. I'm so out of shape. Ugh.

Dr. Marianne wanted to know about my medical insurance. She was most concerned about getting paid and that pissed me off. I had major medical insurance because Mom and Dad insisted that I buy some kind of health insur-

*ance after I graduated college. Wanting to assert my finan-
cial independence, I bought what I could afford to pay for
monthly, which was only major hospitalization. No, the
doctor visits would not be covered and Mom had to assure
the doctor that she would pay my bills.*

*As if that wasn't degrading enough, the nurse then
drew my blood. I screamed. Oh God, I hated needles! The
one good thing about my fear of needles is that it kept me
from ever experimenting with drugs. I'm such a baby. Well,
that concluded the exam. Man, was I glad when my ordeal
was done. I couldn't wait to get out of there.*

It was obvious that Dee Dee was not happy with the
doctor. Under the circumstances, I did not think that any
doctor would have appealed to her. Part of the problem was
that she was accustomed to our kind and caring Dr. Ted.

Dr. Marianne was very cold and clinical. She explained that the blood work, which would be available in a
few days, would give us Dee Dee's T-cell (CD 4) count. I
learned another lesson about HIV: the T-cells protect our
immune system by recognizing foreign invaders and sending
the message to other parts of our immune system to mount a
defense against them. HIV gets into the T-cells and literally
reprograms the cells so they are unable to recognize harmful
germs. So actually it's not the HIV that kills but all the illnesses resulting from the crippled immune system.

The doctor explained that the subsequent infections
are called opportunistic infections or, in HIV lingo, OIs
(pronounced *oh, eyes*). Dr. Marianne told Dee Dee she was
fortunate. Most women are diagnosed when they are pregnant, if diagnosed at all. She told Dee Dee she was lucky
that it was 1993 not 1983. Research had produced so many
treatments for the OIs. She told Dee Dee about AZT (Retro-
vir), DDI (Videx) and DDC (Hivid) now available to treat
HIV. Those drugs were only the beginning of an arsenal of
effective drugs to come. In the 1980s, she said, all she could
do was to tell her patients to go home and prepare to die.
Dee Dee's future was much more hopeful.

We were exhausted and overwhelmed from the appointment. On the drive home, Dee Dee, my chatterbox, was silent. I knew there was nothing I could say to ease her pain.

Later that evening, Denise's brother called. Max talked with Dee Dee for over an hour. During their conversation he suggested that she call *Project Inform* in San Francisco and order their packet of information.

His conversation ended with perhaps the best advice anyone could have given her. "Take real good care of yourself so you can be here for the cure! And, be sure to exercise, take vitamins and reduce the stress in your life."

After talking to someone with HIV, Dee Dee was transformed. Friends could only sympathize with her, while Max really knew what she was going through. More importantly, he began to answer many of her questions.

April 18, 1993

I quickly found out that waiting for test results was one of the most exasperating things about being HIV positive. On my second visit to Dr. Marianne several days later, I learned I had only 75 T-cells! A normal person has 500 to 1500. At 200 T-cells a person is diagnosed with AIDS. I couldn't believe it. Why was this happening to me? How long did I have to live? Why had I met Al, fallen in love and gotten my diagnosis all in the same year?

To add misery to an already miserable situation, Dr. Marianne said that I had to start taking Bactrim, a sulfur-based antibiotic, immediately. She told me never to miss a dose. She further explained that Bactrim is given to someone with AIDS to prevent them from getting PCP (Pneumonia), one of those nasty OIs. I told her that I had just had a bad allergic reaction to Bactrim a couple of weeks ago when I was on tour. She said that she would be attending an HIV seminar that weekend. She would ask the experts if there were any drug that I could substitute for it. Meanwhile, she gave me a prescription for AZT and DDC, two antiretroviral drugs used to attack the HIV. This all began to sound like some kind of nightmarish alphabet soup. (Later, it inspired

Al to write the song The HIV Acronym Blues. *You have to be HIV positive to get the joke.)*

Dr. Marianne called me on Monday and said there wasn't a better prophylactic treatment for PCP than Bactrim. I had no choice but to take it. She would order the desensitizing program at the pharmacy right away.

"Swell," I thought. "No honeymoon for me. No grace period of just being HIV positive. Don't pass go or collect $200. Go straight to AIDS! And, while you're at it, put your body on some nasty sulfur-based drug. Oh God, why me?"

At that time there was only one pharmacy in Dallas where HIV medication was available. It was located in the heart of the gay community about 15 miles away from where we lived. It surprised me when the kind pharmacist offered to drive to our home with the desensitizing medication. After he arrived, he gently talked Dee Dee through the program and assured her it would work. He had done the program successfully with numerous patients. Dee Dee questioned him about the dosages of AZT and DDC. She asked him if they should not be different for her, a small woman. There was no difference in the dosing schedule even though those doses had been determined by testing 150-pound men. The pharmacist helped Dee Dee step into the HIV drug world we later came to call "Better Living through Chemistry."

Later that week, the packet of leaflets arrived from *Project Inform*. We both read them from cover to cover and found them extremely helpful. We learned about transmission, HIV symptoms and about opportunistic infections. The picture was getting pretty ugly—cancer, dementia, blindness and wasting. I did not want to think about those horrible complications. My burning question, for which there was no answer, how was I going to live through all of this to bury my baby?

After reading about HIV symptoms in women— chronic yeast infections, fatigue, unexplained rashes, mollescum, abnormal Pap smears and unexplained fevers—I realized that Dee Dee had all of them. The only doctor who had suggested to Dee Dee that she needed to take an HIV test was the doctor in Lima, Ohio. When he examined her in the ER, he saw thrush in her mouth. He told her thrush appears in babies or people with compromised immune systems. He recommended she get tested for HIV. At that time she and Al laughed and thought it was a ludicrous thing to say.

Given her limited sexual experiences, the fact that she had been a virgin until she was 21 and had had only four partners before Al, they both thought the doctor was way off base. When she returned home, however, she decided to ask our family doctor to run an HIV test. How had everyone else missed it? She had symptoms for eighteen months. No one, not her doctors in New York or her doctors in Dallas caught it. Why? Because, AIDS does not look like that cute, little girl next door. She was not gay or promiscuous or an intravenous drug user. She just did not fit the stereotype!

April 20, 1993

After I read all that stuff from Project Inform, I realized how badly misdiagnosed women were. None of my doctors suggested that I take an HIV test. That really pissed me off. My ideas were forming. Somehow I had to reach other young people especially women and warn them. I also realized that for as long as possible, I had to ward off those nasty opportunistic infections. My immune system will need all the help I can give it. I will take better care of myself. I know that there is no cure for HIV.

In a matter of weeks, I observed a major transformation in Dee Dee. She began to feel a little better physically and emotionally. The desensitizing program was going well. She talked to Al and Marie daily and those calls buoyed her spirits. She looked forward to separate visits from them as soon as they were able to make their flight arrangements. Even when Dee Dee's hair started to fall out in clumps and the doctor wasn't very sympathetic, Dee Dee dealt with it.

With everything happening to her, my daughter accepted her fate faster than any of us could.

During those first few weeks Dee Dee and I decided to go downtown to the AIDS Resource Center. We took an informative AIDS 101 class and began our quest to gather as much information about HIV as we could. At the end of the evening, the instructor passed out dildos and condoms and paired us into teams. There was a contest to see which team could correctly put the condom on the dildo first. We were the only mother/daughter team in the room. And, we won the contest. We laughed and it felt good to laugh. It was our first laugh together since the diagnosis. It was a tiny sign that we were beginning to live with AIDS. On the ride home, I silently thought, "If only I had known about that course when Dee Dee was a teenager and would have taken it with her. Why was I so naïve?"

Chapter Five

SO THIS IS LOVE
May-June 1993

One of the best things that happened to Dee Dee during those initial weeks following her diagnosis was Al's visit to Dallas. Shortly after he arrived at our home, my husband took him upstairs for a private sit-down chat.

"Al, I would certainly understand if you want to bail out of this relationship with my daughter. All I ask is, if you are going to do it, do it now rather than later," Howard exerted his paternal authority.

Al told him that he had no intention of abandoning Dee Dee. He said that he would not do that to any friend of his under these circumstances. Howard felt somewhat relieved, but was not convinced that Al was telling him all that he needed to know. We learned later that during his visit, Al proposed marriage to Dee Dee and she turned him down.

May 1, 1993

When Al proposed to me, I was shocked. I love him so much but I had to say no. I don't want to burden him with my problems. I feel like damaged goods. I so desperately wanted to be self-sufficient before I married anyone. Oh God, I want my life back! This is all so confusing. Then there are my parents. What am I going to do about them? God, what am I supposed to do? Why is all of this happening to me? I can't make any sense of it.

I know I disappointed Al when I refused to marry him. Ever since he has returned to the tour, he seems even more determined to convince me to say yes. He sends me cards, little gifts and love notes every day. We talk on the phone constantly. He is just the kind of guy I have been looking for all of my life. Why, God, why now?

I can't understand why he hasn't gotten his HIV test results either. Damn those two labs he has used on the road. They both screwed up his tests.

May 20, 1993

I was in Miami with my parents visiting with cousins when I learned Al's status. He told me over the phone that he tested positive. I nearly dropped the receiver. Oh God, did I infect him or did he infect me? And, how's it possible? We always used condoms. I cannot believe it. He said that it didn't matter. He loved me and asked me to marry him again. His status changed the whole situation for me. I did not want him to be alone. I demurely said, "yes."

When Dee Dee gave us her permission, cousins in Miami were among the first people that we told that she had AIDS. We were going to be staying in their home and if they were uncomfortable about it, I had to know ahead of time. Their house was Dee Dee's second home when she attended the University of Miami. I was lucky that my cousins were educated about HIV. They had no qualms and wanted us to stay with them.

After we arrived and in total privacy, my cousin, who had always been brutally honest with me, said, "Pat, aren't you angry at her?"

"No," I told her with a puzzled look on my face.

"Well, I am. And I believe she needs to tell you how sorry she is for what she has done to you."

"Done to me?" I was dumbfounded by her remark.
It took me years to realize I felt any anger over this tragedy and, oddly enough, there were very few moments when the anger was directed at my daughter. At one low point I re-

member thinking, "How could Dee Dee be so stupid?" But I never expected her to apologize to me for anything. My pain ran the gamut from disappointment to worry to sadness, but anger would be so counterproductive.

May 25, 1993

So, who infected whom and how did we figure that one out? After I returned to Dallas from Miami, I decided to write to three of the four sexual partners that I had had before I met Al. I simply informed them that I tested positive for HIV and hoped that they would get tested and let me know the results of their tests. There was one fellow, Ethan (not his real name), to whom I could not write. He lived in New York but I didn't know his address.

Al contacted his past partners. They told him that they tested negative. Al had a negative HIV test the year before the tour. Having been a bachelor for several years before we met, occasionally he would get tested. It didn't take us long to conclude that I had probably infected Al.

Most heterosexual guys think that they can't get infected from an HIV positive woman. Well, they better wise up! It happened to us. This is how we think that it happened. Al had dental surgery over the tour hiatus during the Christmas holidays. After I returned to the tour in January, we used condoms faithfully for genital intercourse, but we did have unprotected oral sex. His strange flu in January probably was when he converted from a negative to positive status.

Did I ever find out who infected me? Well, not exactly. In my mind, I eliminated a bad date I experienced while attending the University of Miami. The three guys I wrote to said they tested negative. So, by process of elimination, I decided it had to be "address unknown" in New York. He was the clean-cut, good-looking heterosexual law student that I met in the Lincoln Center Library right after I moved to the city. Looks sure can be deceiving. I hate to admit it, but he was a one-night stand. I had never done anything like that before or since. I was so embarrassed by my behavior. When Ethan called me several times after that evening for another date, I turned him down. About six weeks later, I got real sick. By the time I got to the clinic near school, they thought that I had had "Scarlet Fever." I ran a real high fever for several days and then I broke out in this horrible rash all over my body. No doubt that was when I went from a negative to a positive HIV status. Then I got odd bumps on my neck. My HIV symptoms started almost immediately.

Dee Dee decided that it would be best to make her home with Al in Denver. Al offered to move to Dallas but Denver was Al's hometown where he had lifelong friends and work-connections. Dee Dee wanted him to be close to his roots and she hoped to find theater work in Denver, too. She was determined to prove to us and to herself that she was grown-up and could take care of herself. She also knew that her brother and his wife lived nearby in Boulder. To her, the move made perfect sense. To me, it did not. After all, she was my baby who was sick.

May 27, 1993
Today Mom gave me this beautiful 14-carat gold "Chai" charm on a chain to wear around my neck. "Chai" is the Hebrew symbol for life. I'm so touched. This charm was given to my mother from Dad's grandma when they got engaged. Mom wore it when she had post-partum depression in her twenties and had to be hospitalized. She feels the charm has mystical, curative powers, but I know that there is no cure for HIV. At a gut level I know that I won't survive this, but I'm determined to live each and every day that God gives me to the fullest. That much I can say with certainty.
Last night I asked my parents if I could meet with their lawyer. I want to do a living will and a directive to physicians before I move to Denver. When my time comes, I don't want to be kept alive on any machines. I know that was too much for my parents to hear at this time.

Then I had a long conversation with Mom and Dad about finances. I told them that I did not want them spending their hard-earned life savings on this disease. I felt that the money they had saved for retirement needed to be there when they retired. I can handle my own life. I plan to work when I get to Denver for as long as possible. Al will work. I will access the public health system. This is my life and this is the way I want to live it!

I remember the discussion with Dee Dee about finances. She was never very practical, but I had to admire her pluck and idealism. She felt that she and Al could support themselves. I confided my frustration to my cousin. He said that I should not worry because opportunities would come along for Howard and me to help her. He was ever so right!

Howard and I took many evening walks during which we discussed endlessly Dee Dee's illness and all its ramifications including the issue of finances.

"Honey, I know that we planned to leave our children an inheritance when we died but what are we going to do now?" I gently treaded in on the subject.

"Dee Dee doesn't want our help financially, at least not right now."

"I know but I feel we need to give it to her now."

"It's funny. But I was thinking the exact same thing! Guess we'll just have to wait for the right opportunities and seize upon them."

It amazes me how we always seem to be of one mind on these matters. We kept alert for opportunities to gift monies to her. When one came along, we did not hesitate to help her or Al, whether it was for something simple like buying groceries or something large like helping them buy their house.

One of my friends gave me this incredible piece of advice after we told her about Dee Dee. Put simply she said, "Make good memories. It's the only thing you can do under these circumstances." Whenever and wherever we could, that is exactly what we did.

Before she left Dallas, Dee Dee, Howard and I attended a women's seminar on HIV. A young lady named Suzanne stepped up to the podium. She started pitching condoms into the audience. She was funny and upbeat as she told her story. Yes, she was HIV positive, and her openness was a breath of fresh air. Dee Dee was very impressed with her. "Mom, I could do that!" I knew that ideas were forming in her mind to go public with her story.

Suzanne belonged to an HIV positive women's support group led by Barbara Cambridge. After the seminar, she invited Dee Dee to come to a meeting. Dee Dee was reluctant to attend because she did not think it would help her. I prodded her to go because I felt she needed the support of other women in her situation. After much pushing, I finally got Dee Dee to agree to attend a meeting. The women she met in the group were older than she was but they were very accepting of her. They laughed a lot and helped each other. When Dee Dee was coping with her adjustment to AZT and her hair loss, it was these women who talked Dee Dee through it. The women in the group told her how to handle annoying phone solicitors who called. "When they ask you how are you today, just tell them that you are dying from AIDS! It's a real show stopper." She tried it and it tickled her fancy every time she heard the phone go...click.

I remembered when Howard's parents were diagnosed with Alzheimer's Disease that we were referred to a support group. We found the group very helpful in guiding us through all the situations we were facing. Now faced with another crisis, I knew we needed the support of others going through similar circumstances. Later that month, I found support from the "Just between Us" support group for parents and/or siblings of people with HIV. My husband and I went together. I'm not sure what we expected that evening when we walked into the meeting room in the Episcopal Church of the Ascension in Dallas, but there were 24 people gathered around a U-shaped table. We were greeted warmly by people who were white, middle-class parents just like us. All of us shared how we were doing and how our children were doing. Some parents were struggling as much with their sons' homosexuality as they were with the HIV. We were the only parents with a heterosexual daughter with AIDS.

While some parents had lost their children, most of us had children in various stages of the disease. The grieving parents, and it didn't matter whether they lost their child a week ago or years earlier, were an inspiration to us. Each person's story was different. Through their experiences, I began to see that there was life after loss. It is from this group that I learned a matter of utmost importance to me, the caregiver: self-care. Over the years I have come to believe that stress and grief profoundly affected the parents who did not take care of themselves. They appeared to suffer more incidences of cancer, heart disease, accidents and divorce. This disease does not just happen to the person who is *infected* with HIV. This disease profoundly impacts the people *affected* by HIV—the people who love someone with the disease.

I was so glad to find the parents support group. The ground rules were simple. What was said in that room, stayed in that room and no one could leave a meeting without a hug. I will be forever indebted to the mother who started the group. After the meeting, I wondered if our Jewish community had a support group like this one. (As I later found out, it did not, but it does now.)

June 3, 1993

The tour ended a few days ago. Al returned to Denver to look for a place for us to live. He called to tell me that he had rented an old Victorian house that needed a little work but was in fairly good shape.

"It's located in a changing neighborhood at the edge of downtown Denver," Al said, expressing his concern about the neighborhood.

"I don't care where we live. I love you. What matters is we will soon be together again." Time was precious and love was all became our mantra.

"Mom's hovering over me again. Last night I spiked a fever and she went into mother-smother overdrive. I need to show her that I'm okay and to prove to her that I'm an adult." I took care of myself in New York and with Al's love, I just know that I can do that again in Denver.

Dee Dee's relocation to Denver caused me the worst case of separation anxiety. Separations from her always made me anxious. I would worry. Would she be okay without my care and watchful eye? How would other people treat her? Would she make good choices and decisions? How would I cope with the loneliness, loss of control and loss of her attention? My anxiety was at the root of too many sleepless nights. But, like the first day of school and the day she left for college or the time she left the country for the Soviet Union or moved to New York, I knew that I had to let her go. My daughter, my baby, had AIDS, but she was a woman who needed to make her home with the man she loved in Denver. Roots and wings.

June 4, 1993

I know that Mom is very worried about me. I promised her that I would call her often. When I lived away in the past, we would touch base about twice a week. I know that this time it's a whole lot different and I'll call her every day.

The best thing I did for Mom was that I released her to share my status with her family and friends. Truthfully, right now I don't care who knows that I have AIDS. Since I've decided to go public with my story, there's no reason for her to keep my secret any longer.

Dee Dee promised to stay in close communication with Howard and me. In addition to a pact to talk with her and Al regularly, we planned frequent visits. Either would visit them in Denver or we would fly them to Dallas or meet them somewhere else. I'm grateful for the diligence both she and Al gave to keeping us well informed and for sharing their journey with us.

My daughter's parting shot as she left Dallas was "You might as well tell everyone now, Mom, because I'm hoping to be on the *Oprah Show* some day. And, I don't think that would be the best way for someone you know to learn that I have AIDS!"

June 15, 1993

After much soul-searching, the only sense I could make out of all of this is that God wants me to use my performance talents to tell others about this horrible disease that is taking the lives of young people like me. Upon my departure, I gave Mom the green light. If I'm going to go public with my story, surely she can go public, too.

Chapter Six

THE BURDEN OF HER SECRET
Summer-Fall 1993

There was so much fear, ignorance and prejudice wrapped around AIDS, it was easy to understand why my daughter did not want me to tell anyone about her situation. During the first three months following her diagnosis, she gradually told her friends and she also allowed me to confide in a few people close to me.

For the most part, however, I lived with the stress of keeping her secret and the resulting isolation I felt from others. At a conscious and unconscious level, I knew the only way for me to survive this thing was to solicit people's support. But I had to honor my daughter's wishes. This was not about me; it was about her. I learned quickly that serious illness is not about the caregiver but the patient.

After Dee Dee moved to Denver, I took my first step in sharing our secret with a wider circle of family and friends. It was one thing to be freed to tell others and another thing to actually do it. It was easy to share my story in the parents support group. After all, those people were strangers and living with similar circumstances. It was another thing altogether to tell the people who knew us intimately and loved Dee Dee and our family. Dee Dee was the one who told my parents and I will never forget how she did it.

A month following Dee Dee's diagnosis, my mother and I got into an argument on the telephone over some trivial matter. I hung up on her, which I had never done before.

Dee Dee was watching this interchange. She then picked up the phone and called her grandma. "Grandma. I've something to tell you. When I do, you'll understand why Mommy was so short with you. Is Grandpa home?"

My father was not home at that time. She asked my mother to call her back when he returned. About an hour later, they returned her call.

"I've something to tell you," she bluntly said to my parents, "I'm HIV positive. We've just found out. I'm doing well and taking real good care of myself."

My parents took the news better than I ever expected considering their ages and the fact that this was not the kind of news any grandparent would want to hear from a grandchild. Of course my mother apologized to me. She knew from the sound of my voice that something was terribly wrong, but she felt she could not ask me what it was. I guess there is not a mother anywhere who cannot tell by the sound of her child's voice when something is wrong no matter how old that child is! And, I did not have a clue how to go about telling my parents such devastating news. I was proud of the courage my daughter displayed.

Back to my challenge: how best to inform others about Dee Dee. Howard recommended that I write a letter to our family and friends who did not live in the Dallas area as a starting place. It sounded reasonable to me. The format of the letter was done in Dee Dee's up-front style. I just laid it out, her diagnosis, state of her health and her treatments. In it I wrote…"we have wrapped her in a stress-free cocoon and are committed to giving Dee Dee the best quality of life…leaving her self-esteem and independence intact."

I told them about Al, the wonderful man who loved her and about their engagement and wedding plans. It was great to have some good news to juxtapose against the bad news. I closed the letter with some information about AIDS and resources for them to read or contact. Without realizing it, I was developing my own platform to educate others about this disease.

Even though the tone of the letter was positive, I was still afraid to mail it. I could not anticipate people's reactions or how I would deal with their reactions. Would they shun Dee Dee or our family? And, I hated to be the bearer of bad news. So I decided to mail the letters, which later became a series of letters, after we left the country for a ten-day trip to Israel. My thinking was simple: give these people time to recover from the shock before they called us.

Dee Dee wanted us to take the trip to Israel that we had scheduled many months before her diagnosis. She assured us that she would be just fine with Al in Denver while we were gone. If I had cancelled the trip, she would have been angry with me.

I was caught in that "damned if you do and damned if you don't" place again. How could I deal with the anxiety of traveling out of the country under these circumstances let alone enjoy myself? At some point it became obvious—I had to do the trip for Dee Dee.

The trip was spiritually uplifting. I placed prayers in the Western Wall in Jerusalem for Dee Dee, for Al, for a healthy grandchild and for my aging parents. I bothered God a lot. What a crazy year, I thought. The roller coaster ride of highs and lows was something I never wanted and found disorienting. The spiritual infusion I experienced in Israel was desperately needed and just wonderful.

When we returned from Israel, I was further uplifted by the responses to my letter. Our loved ones dissolved my fears of rejection with their warm response of support. And, the more people who knew our secret, the less isolated I felt and the lower my stress level became.

Upon returning home, the first thing I did was phone my daughter. She sounded very happy. She and Al had become officially engaged a few days after her arrival in Denver and they began talking about the wedding. I worried about the pressure of planning a wedding. Would it be too much for her? I worried about whether she would be well enough to enjoy her wedding. Would she live long enough to celebrate her own wedding?

June 18, 1993

    Shortly after I moved to Denver, Al gave me a ring. He planned this romantic picnic on a beautiful mountain. Only, I was having so much trouble adjusting to the altitude in Colorado that he had to settle for a less romantic spot. He placed the ring, a diamond that belonged to my grandma, on my finger and pledged his eternal love. I can't stop looking at it. It's hard to believe that I am engaged.

June 25, 1993

    I read in the Rocky Mountain News *that the* Theater on Broadway *was holding auditions for a Kander and Ebb musical,* And the World Goes 'Round. *I told Al I wanted to audition for a role. He understood my need to establish myself as a performer in the Denver arts community. It was the work that I knew and loved.*

    I was thrilled to be cast in the show. It was especially wonderful that Al was hired as the music director. We would be working together again. I knew I was pushing it. The rehearsals would be exhausting but I was determined not to give up my life. My health was pretty good now even though I was still struggling with fatigue, mouth ulcers and yeast infections. Well, that's not life threatening.

    I want to look for part-time work with children because I just love kids. I can't spend my time worrying about every little germ. Al convinced me, however, that daily exposure to groups of kids isn't such a smart thing for me to do right now. I know he's right but it really hurts. Guess I can't whine about it. 'Cause only I'm responsible for the mess I've made of my life!

    Near the end of August that summer, after my successful letter writing campaign, it was time to tell our Dallas "family" about Dee Dee. I decided that the best way to do it was to hold a series of three informal coffees in our home.

Our close friends were invited and told that we needed to play catch-up on what had been happening in our lives during that summer. Dee Dee thought this was hilarious, and she dubbed those evenings "Mom's HIV Coffees."

Howard and I gathered our friends into our living room and Howard started. He told them our horrific news. I just could not do it. Then we told them our "good" news—the engagement and impending wedding. We shared with them some information about HIV, making the assumption that our friends were uneducated about the disease. Surprisingly, many were already well informed.

Like circus performers, our emotions danced on a high wire. Would we fall? Would we become victims of AIDS? Most of our friends broke down and cried. We held each other. There were questions. We answered them. By the end of the evening, it was hard to tell who was supporting whom, but we were glad that we had shared the burden of our secret. I asked for people's confidentiality for a couple of more weeks while we completed our round of coffees and then they could tell anyone. Oddly enough, most people only talked to the immediate members of their families about it, which surprised us.

As painful as it was to do the coffees, it was easier for me to cope with my crisis after I widened my circle of support. Time and again, friends asked me, "How were you able to handle this crisis without falling apart?" What they didn't realize was that they were the very reason I was able to survive. Each person in his or her own way was carrying me. Besides, the option of falling apart was not there. My daughter needed me. My husband needed me. My family needed me. My friends needed me. So, I was determined to do whatever it would take for me to stay well.

A short course in self-care: If the caretaker doesn't take care of herself, then who will? And, more importantly, who will be there for the patient? So, what did I do to take care of myself? I prayed, doubled my vitamin C, exercised, talked, used massage therapy, sang, kept a journal, did talk therapy, saw my internist regularly, took a mild antidepressant and stayed active, busy and involved. But, most importantly, I prayed.

With it all, during those first six months, I was just going through the motions of living. All of the joy of life was gone. It was as if a monster vacuum cleaner had run over me and everywhere there was any potential for happiness, it sucked it up.

On October 1, 1993 I experienced one of life's most blessed events: the birth of my first grandson, Benjamin. Dee Dee was with him shortly after he entered the world. Excited to become "Aunt Dee Dee," she called me immediately to share her joy. Her happiness was infectious, just like her glorious smile. A few weeks later, we traveled to Colorado to meet our newest family member. A good friend told me once that a grandchild is the only thing in this life that is not overrated and I could not agree with her more.

When I returned to Dallas, I felt renewed. The joy experienced from holding my son's firstborn son, this new life, made me feel that the circle of life was completed. I realized life goes on. Three weeks later I emotionally "woke up" one morning. I looked at myself in the mirror and said, "Is your cup half full or half empty?" I decided that I had to count my blessings. Both of my children were happy. My son was a father. My daughter was engaged. My husband and I were grandparents of a healthy grandson. We had just been to visit our homeland, Israel. We had incredibly wonderful friends and family. At that moment I decided I would not let HIV continue to cast a black shadow over all that was good about my life. Was there a hole in my heart? Yes. It was a cavernous crater, but I was determined to move forward by filling that hole with life's blessings!

Chapter Seven

THE WORLD KEEPS SPINNING
Summer-Fall 1993

Part of the plan that made our physical separation from Dee Dee easier to bear involved frequent trips to Denver. Howard and I took the first of those too-numerous-to-count trips in July. This time we would celebrate my 51st birthday with just our family.

To say that the contrast between this year and last year was enormous would be an understatement. How had I known that I needed this past year away from the world of daily work? I told Howard that it would be very difficult for me to return to work full-time and cope with our family crisis. He understood, so we decided to leave my work-related activities the same for awhile.

Over the last several months, I had met many parents whose adult-children had HIV. Each person had a different way of coping with the crisis. Some parents found that their jobs and working were actually their salvation. The busier they kept themselves, the better they felt. Others could not focus well enough to work. For many people there were no options—work or do not eat. I was one of the lucky ones. I had a choice. For me, the epicenter of my life had to be my daughter.

This was our first trip to Denver since Dee Dee's diagnosis and I did not observe any marked physical changes in her, but it had only been a month since she had moved from Dallas. It was a bonus for Howard and me to take one flight and be able to visit both of our children. It had been many years since our children lived so close to each other.

On the evening of my birthday we all met for dinner in the Boulderado Hotel in Boulder. What a gift: the sight of my husband, my son, my daughter-in-law blooming with my first grandchild, my daughter and my future son-in-law all together for the celebration of my birthday!

June 30, 1993

As part of getting settled in my new digs, Al and I feathered our nest. The house needed some paint and repairs but to me it felt like a mansion. My last home was a four-room apartment in New York City shared with three other actresses. I didn't mind the neighborhood in Denver. So what if an occasional wino walked past our house? I saw much worse on the streets of New York. This house was a huge step up from my City apartment. We had so much space and, for all of it, we paid one-third of the rent of the New York apartment. We needed to buy some furnishings and to hang some pictures on our walls to make the place homey. Savoring the delicious moment, I busied myself with shopping at yard sales and assembling some accent pieces from silk flowers that I purchased at our local craft store. It was exciting and I was having a fun time. I even surprised Al who was impressed with my creative talents and my thriftiness. Best of all it felt like I was on a vacation from HIV.

Some of the houses in Dee Dee and Al's neighborhood were beautifully restored and others were in terrible need of repair. In my opinion, their rental house fell somewhere in the middle. While the outside of the house appeared newly painted and repaired, the inside did need some attention. Keeping within a tight budget, Dee Dee and Al purchased a few pieces of furniture. Dee Dee was so proud of an antique dining room table and chairs that she found at a local yard sale. She planned to recover the seats on the chairs and to refinish the table some day. Al cleaned out all of the flowerbeds and trimmed the bushes. What impressed me the most, though, were not the physical things they did to make their house a home. Their home was aglow with their love—filled with music—their special bond. The romance of candles and fresh flowers warmed their dining room that day and every day as I soon came to learn.

AIDS was not forgotten. In addition to seeing the house, Dee Dee had arranged for Howard and me to meet with her doctor and nurse practitioner. Our daughter was intuitive and hoped that by introducing us to her medical team, it would lower our anxiety about her medical care. I looked forward to the meeting and appreciated the opportunity she gave me to be a part of her new life.

July 2, 1993

One of the first things I did after I moved to Denver was to access the public health system. My health insurance only covered major hospitalization, and the majority of my care would be outpatient visits. The clinic was on the campus of Denver General Hospital, just a short car ride from our rental house.

At the Infectious Disease Clinic, I learned about Colorado AIDS Project. I don't know what Al and I would have done if it had not been for all the wonderful organizations the gay community had established for people like us living with HIV. I was so impressed with the warm way they welcomed us at CAP even though we were a heterosexual couple. I don't understand why people in the heterosexual world fear and shun the gay community.

My decision to access the public health system wasn't only a financial one. In 1993, Denver General was the best place for an HIV patient in Denver because they handled so many HIV cases.

I couldn't decide what was worse—the needle sticks for the blood draws I got at every visit or sitting in the clinic waiting area with all the really sick patients. It was scary. I thought about this before I brought Mom and Dad to the clinic to meet Dr. Judy and my nurse practitioner, Patty. I tried to forewarn them. I did not want them to look at the patients with pity because I never wanted anyone to feel sorry for me. I felt relieved on the day we went to the clinic because we didn't see anyone on an IV or in the final stages of AIDS.

I marveled at how comfortable Dee Dee was in the Denver General I.D. clinic. In a matter of just a few weeks, she knew everyone in the clinic and everyone greeted her by her name when she checked in. Dee Dee worked the system well. Her doctor and nurse earned my highest admiration for their work with AIDS patients. After our meeting, I felt blessed that they both showed such a special interest in my daughter's welfare. The women were kind and caring yet firm when treating her. I left the clinic feeling relieved knowing that Dee Dee was in such good hands.

July 10, 1993
In some odd way, my whole life feels like it has been a rehearsal for this new phase of my life. I have lived almost every day not feeling well. To understand this, I guess you have to take a look at me when I was a little baby: I gently and easily slid into this world at 1:00 A.M. on September 19, 1968 in Jefferson Hospital in Philadelphia. Born with a lot of mucous, my doctor immediately put me in the preemie nursery for a 24-hour stay, until I was breathing better. My bedmates were all tiny babies. At six pounds eight ounces and 19 inches long, I was a gentle giant. This was the only time in my entire life that I ever was physically bigger than my peers were. Mom saw me for the first time in that nursery and she was so relieved that I was the healthiest looking baby. I gazed at her with my big round eyes. I was lucky to be born into this ready-made family...a mommy, a daddy and a brother, who was bragging to everyone he met that he had a new baby sister. So, who cares that I had a little cold?
During my first few months of life, Mommy told me I was frequently sick either with colds or ear infections. She was forever putting salve on my skin rashes.

My health didn't improve when I became a toddler. If there was any bug going around, I caught it. If my brother, Alan, caught it, he would be sick for three or four days. Me, I'd be down for ten days. To make matters worse, every time I got sick, I'd lose weight. Mom said I was so skinny I looked like a plucked chicken. I weighed only 17 pounds at a year. Most babies with my birth weight would have weighed 20 pounds by their first birthday. By age two, I still only weighed 17 pounds. Obviously, I was sick a lot during my second year of life, too. Mom said my saving grace was I was a smiley, talkative, upbeat child even when I was sick.

I was three years old when the family moved from Cherry Hill, New Jersey to Dallas, Texas. After we got settled, Mom had me tested for allergies and, sure enough, there were many things I was allergic to. I was treated with a variety of pills and given an inhaler to help me breathe. Still, I woke up most mornings feeling sick. For many years I would start my day with going to the toilet to gag up mucous. Not a fun way to start a day, but I came to accept it as part of my morning ritual. As a result I never cared much for breakfast and on many mornings, I also had little or no desire to go to school.

Long before Dee Dee was infected with HIV, she had a compromised immune system. I suspect that she probably had half as many T-cells as the average person did when she became infected. I am also convinced that her sickly youth somehow contributed to her rapid decline though I do not have any clinical proof. And, it cannot be overlooked that her doctors misdiagnosed her symptoms. We learned the hard way that an early diagnosis is paramount to long-term survival with HIV, as is the importance of getting tested after participation in any risky behavior.

June 28, 1993

Now that I'm living in Denver, I need to buy a car. When I moved to New York, I sold my car to Patrick, my good friend from college, because I didn't need one in the City. I want to buy a used car, but Mom and Dad insist that I buy a new one. In order to do this my parents will have to sign on a car loan. They've agreed to do it. All I can afford to pay is one-third of the monthly car payment. They offered to pay the other two-thirds. I have mixed feelings about this. On the one hand, it will be very exciting to have a new car, but on the other hand, I want to be financially independent and now I won't be. I relented and we took out a four-year loan. Funny, I doubt if I'll live long enough to see the loan paid off. I bought a red Honda Civic and named her "Roxy" after my role in the show Chicago *that I did in college.*

I'm looking forward to Mom and Dad's visit in a few days. I want them to meet Roxy and to see all the decorating I've done in the house. Al and I planted flowers in the front yard yesterday and it looks pretty. My folks are bringing a mezuzah, a little decorative box encasing a tiny Hebrew scroll Jews affix to the doorpost of their homes. We're going to ceremonially affix one by our front door. That will be the finishing touch...our house will then be "home."

We were happy to help Dee Dee buy a new car. Howard and I felt a new car would be safer and less problematic for her than a used one would be. Al owned one of his old "throw away" cars named "Old Blue." When his cars became a problem, he just got rid of them. I felt better knowing that at least one of their cars would provide reliable transportation, especially under the circumstances.

I had to trust that Dee Dee knew what she was doing when she accessed the public health system in Denver. Even though I wanted her in private care, she would not allow it because she knew that we would have to pay for it. When Howard and I met Dr. Judy and Patty, her nurse practitioner, we opened a channel of communication between us. I gave gave Dee Dee's medical team our telephone numbers. We wanted them to be comfortable calling us if they needed us. I felt encouraged after our first meeting because we had established some rapport.

Dee Dee explained to us that even though the hospital and the clinic were both Denver General, they were not exactly connected. If Dee Dee would be hospitalized, she would be dealing with different doctors, but her doctor would be consulted and have visiting privileges.

Dee Dee had some very definite ideas about treating her HIV. She was opposed to participating in any clinical trials because, at that time, women were not included in the initial research. She read that the testing had been done on 150-pound men and it bothered her because she was a 90-pound woman. She often questioned even the FDA-approved drugs and drug dosage schedules. She told me she felt like a guinea pig and, in many ways, she was.

She learned about compassionate care drug programs available from some of the large pharmaceutical companies. Through these programs, drug companies made some of their medications available to people like her, who could not afford to buy them, or to people who needed them before they were available in the general marketplace.

When Dee Dee moved to Denver she was taking both AZT and DDC. Dr. Judy advised Dee Dee to eliminate the DDC. At that time, none of the research indicated that there was any advantage to doing combo therapy (more than one drug) over the monotherapy (taking only one drug at a time). Today, in the age of HIV "cocktails," research has proven the efficacy of taking at least three drugs at the same time to treat HIV. Next to her anemia and general deterioration from AZT, my daughter's biggest problem was her dwindling weight—nothing new for her, but of greater concern in the setting of AIDS.

June 30, 1993

I've never been a scale watcher because my weight has never been an issue for me. Most of my girlfriends were constantly on diets and the scale. I even had a friend in high school that had anorexia. When I was a teenager, I asked Mom if I had anorexia. She laughed and said no, I was just one of those lucky few who was naturally thin. In the world of HIV, I quickly learned that being thin was not so lucky a thing to be!

At every clinic visit, I dreaded getting on the scale. It was a struggle to keep my weight up. It didn't help that I was singing and dancing in World Goes 'Round. *One of the numbers from the show even had me tap dancing on roller skates. Mouth sores made it difficult for me to eat. My nurse would send me to the dietician and she would give me these nutritional drinks. I tried them and all they did was fill me up so much that I couldn't eat at mealtimes.*

Another problem I had was HIV anemia, one of the side effects of AZT. Dr. Judy said she would treat the anemia with either Epo (Epoetin) shots or an occasional blood transfusion—more needles. Later, I took a small squishy stuffed red bear with me to squeeze when I got a needle stick. Believe it or not, after awhile I got to the point where the needles didn't even bother me.

I think AZT is responsible for my thinning hair. It's growing stringier looking daily. It's a good thing that I'm not a vain person or I might become severely depressed. The worst of this whole thing is the fatigue. I used to be such a dynamo. I could have done eight shows a week with energy to spare. Now I'll be lucky to get through four shows a week of World Goes 'Round *for a four-week run with going to bed for the entire day following each show. My life...my life...I want my life back!*

In September, I traveled to Denver without Howard to see Dee Dee's show. I was shocked by the physical changes in her after only two months from our last visit. The image of her when she stepped onto the stage to do her first, and pivotal, number in *World Goes 'Round* will forever be etched in my memory. She had that AIDS look—sunken eyes and hollow cheeks. In the opening scene, Dee Dee is leaning against a lamppost, the lighting is dim as she sings the song, *But the World Goes 'Round*. My heart hurt to see how rail thin she had become. She looked frail, but she could still belt a torch song. My daughter was singing and dancing in the face of AIDS! I could not believe her steely resolve.

Following the performance that evening, Dee Dee and Al held a small party in their home. They had invited some of their friends over to help her celebrate her 25th birthday. They always filled their home with friends, lots of friends. As I prepared for bed that evening I wondered, "How many more birthdays will she get to celebrate?"

The next day we talked about her wedding. She and Al had chosen the Phipps Tennis Pavilion in Denver for both the ceremony and reception site and booked it for March 6, 1994. She often said she chose March because it made the wedding feel like it would take place "later." They took me to see the facility. It was a beautiful room that looked like a huge indoor garden. Then we visited a caterer and a stationer. After just those few stops, we had to quit. My daughter was too tired to go any further. It pained me to see her moving so slowly. My youthful daughter with her boundless energy was gone.

This was supposed to be a high time of my life but it was agonizing. I would lie awake at night praying to God, "Please let Dee Dee live long enough to have her wedding," as tears rolled softly down my cheeks.

Planning Dee Dee's wedding made me feel so conflicted. I worried, "Could she handle the stress?" She wanted to be in charge, but I knew that she was the grand master at procrastination. Dee Dee wanted a beautiful, traditional wedding with all the trimmings. It required many hours of planning to have that kind of wedding. I just could not deny her wishes. Not wanting her to be too sick to enjoy her day, I walked a tightrope, gently nudging her along but trying not to put her under too much pressure.

I returned to Dallas from that trip with an aching heart. Dee Dee challenged me about putting the wedding plans in place so early and she resisted doing it, but needless to say, I persisted. As we contracted each businessperson, we also notified them about her illness. "The bride has AIDS and the groom is HIV positive"—certainly not your usual scenario for a bridal couple. Most of the service people were very understanding and said that they would make allowances if it became necessary.

In my opinion, Dee Dee had enough to do between planning the wedding and doing the show. Then she called to tell me that she had auditioned for and got cast in a children's theater production of *Wind in the Willows* for the Shwayder Theater. Her rehearsals would start while she was performing *World Goes 'Round,* but she did not see it as any problem—just a small overlap of a few performances.

"Dee Dee, how can you do both shows at once?"

"No problem, Mom." That was my Dee Dee. Nothing was going to stop her from performing.

October 16, 1993

I know Mom thought I was crazy when I called to tell her I had taken the role of Mole in Wind in the Willows, *but I wanted to work. Maybe this wasn't a good decision. I promised Mom that Al and I would take a little vacation between the shows. A long weekend trip to San Diego for some rest and relaxation sounded just perfect. Mom and Dad sent us the money for the trip.*

Well, World Goes 'Round *got an extended run in the Springs, which I did not anticipate. If I had known that I wouldn't have auditioned for* Wind in the Willows. *But I was already committed. Remember, in one of the numbers from* World Goes 'Round, *I was tap dancing on roller skates. Doing two shows simultaneously added to my dwindling weight problem. My doctor kept threatening to put me in the hospital if my weight fell below 85 pounds. I struggled to keep those 85 pounds on me. I even drank those lousy nutritional drinks. Ugh, gag me. And I doubled the clothing that I wore on the days that I had to weigh in at the clinic. I don't think that I was fooling anybody.*

November 10, 1993

The trip to San Diego was refreshing. We rested and walked on the beach. We made love, always using a condom so Al would not get infected with my HIV strain, which was probably more virulent than the one he had.

On a lark, we visited a psychic while we were there. I was a total stranger to her and I was careful not to tell her anything about myself. First she told me I had been an Indian woman with nine children in a previous life, which is why I would not have any children in this life. She hit on the one thing that bothered me the most about having AIDS— that I would never have any children of my own. Then the psychic said something to me that was really weird. She said, "It is time for you to hang up your skates!" How did she know that I was tap dancing on roller skates? I didn't give it a whole lot of thought, until after I returned to Denver.

During my next performance of Wind in the Willows, *I had an attack of diarrhea while ON STAGE. I ran off to the restroom. Fortunately the other actors covered my lines. When the show was over I said to Al, "That's it! After this show's run, no more performance theater for me. I've decided to hang up my skates!"*

It wasn't easy for me to give up doing theater; it had been my dream ever since I was a little girl. I was only 25. Angry and frustrated, I turned those feelings into the motivation I needed to do my AIDS presentations. The message was clear—do something about this horrible disease!

Chapter Eight

GOING PUBLIC
Fall 1993

August 1, 1993
I had my first thoughts about going public with my story after attending a women's HIV seminar with Mom and Dad in Dallas. A young woman stood before the audience and inspired me with her story. After I moved to Denver, Al and I had lengthy discussions about going public. We were both performers and we knew we could hold an audience. All we needed to do was educate ourselves about HIV and prepare a presentation with some visual aids. Al agreed to do the technical, medical stuff. That pleased me since I wasn't scientifically oriented anyway.

When we registered at CAP, I asked my counselor how we could get on their speakers' bureau. He said that he would call us later when the speaking season got closer. Apparently many schools are interested in AIDS programs in the weeks prior to World AIDS Day—December 1.

Last night we saw a wonderful production of Fiddler on the Roof *done by PHAMILY, which is a group of physically handicapped performers. After the show I met one of the actors, Lucy. She has severe Parkinson's disease at 32. She keeps herself active in the Denver arts community on her good days. I know that we'll become good friends. She told us that her cousin and many of her friends have died from AIDS. She was so touched by our story.*

*When the planners of the Colorado AIDS Walk
called Lucy she said, "You have the wrong person. You need
to call Dee Dee and Al." When we were invited to speak in
Lucy's place, I just knew the AIDS Walk was the right time
and place for us to launch our public life.*

September 5, 1993
    *We weren't sure what to say the first time we spoke to
the crowd of 8000 walkers who gathered in Cheesman Park
for the AIDS Walk. Very simply, we told them who we were
and that we were HIV positive. We thanked the crowd for
coming and told them how grateful we were to have their
support. We sang, "Somewhere Over the Rainbow." Al prepared a track of the song on his synthesizer and we used the
track for our accompaniment. Al sang the introduction. I
sang the song, and we did the reprise together. We chose
that song because both Judy Garland, who made the song
famous, and the song itself were popular with the gay community. It was very much against type for me to sing a song
that was so strongly identified with any performer, especially
someone who did it so magnificently. But selecting the right
song for the moment was more important to me than my own
desire to make an impression as a performer. I always chose
music that spoke to my audience and this time I had a
pressing need to inspire the crowd.*
    *I was enthralled by the crowd of walkers and being
on the same dais with Pat Schroeder, our state representative. After the performance I felt like a star-struck teen when
I told Pat that she was my hero and how much I admired her.
She turned to me and said, "No, Dee Dee, it is YOU who is
the hero for disclosing your status and for what you are doing for other women."*
    *We were "out" in the community and soon affection-
ately became known as "that cute, HIV positive, heterosexual
couple." Channel 4 television was the station that covered
the walk and one of their reporters asked to interview us.
After the interview aired, calls for other interviews started
flooding into our home.*

I granted one of my first interviews with the Denver Jewish Post. *I was shocked when they ran my story by giving me the anonymous name of Sandy. I called the editor and registered my complaint. "I have nothing to hide," I yelled at him. I hated all the secrecy around this disease. He told me that he did it to protect my family in Dallas. I said, "Bull----. My parents are open about my status, too." Obviously, I didn't get very far with this editor. But, I learned a bitter lesson about dealing with the media. After they interview you, they pretty much have the freedom to write what they want. There is no controlling how the media will present your story. Al and I were on our way to becoming local celebrities—an odd sort of fame.*

How did I feel about Dee Dee speaking publicly? Put simply, I was proud of her. I never saw any reason to hide the fact that she had AIDS or how she became infected. It made me angry when parents of gay young men said to me, "Well, it's different for you since your daughter is not gay. A heterosexual person with AIDS and a gay person with AIDS is like the difference between being a widow and a divorcée." They implied that my circumstances were less of an embarrassment because of the stigma attached to being gay. I just could not agree. To me, AIDS was a disease not a lifestyle. It is so sad that this disease came into the United States through the gay community because it got bogged down in morality and political issues. In the rest of the world, AIDS is predominantly in the heterosexual community with the majority of people infected being heterosexual women.

September 15, 1993
Now that Al and I had media attention, we knew we would be called upon to speak to groups. I had to prepare my statement. I wanted to be totally honest so I knew that I had to disclose something that had always been very private to me, my sex life. I called Marie in New York and asked her to help me. "Marie, you are such a wonderful writer, can you write my statement for me?"

"Dee Dee, you can do this better than anyone else. Speak from your heart. Just tell them your story. What would you want to know if you were in that audience?"

"I'd want to know how the speaker became infected with HIV."

"Good. Now what will you say to them so they understand who you are and how you became infected?"

"I guess I'll have to tell the story of my life including my sex life. But you know what, Marie? I don't care who knows what I did or why I did it."

"Exactly. So what is your message?"

"I especially want other young women to stand up for themselves and not wind up where I am because they were too embarrassed to tell their partner to use a condom. I want them to understand that they do have choices. In fact that's what I'll title my presentation, 'Choices.' Thanks, Marie, once again, you've been a big help!"

I really wanted Marie to write my statement, but in the end I'm glad that she didn't. Al and I talked for many nights about our presentation. We theater people do our best work at night. He reminded me that I looked like a teenager and I'd have a natural "in" with the young females in my audience. Al, because he was older, thought that he'd have a harder time connecting with the guys. He was right. After most of our talks, the girls in the audience would gather around me. Al nicknamed me "Velcro Legs."

I decided to title our presentation "Choices" because I sincerely believed if we gave the young people in our audiences the correct information, then they could make an informed choice. For some people, that would mean choosing abstinence, which, I always emphasized, was the safest thing to do. But for those who chose not to be abstinent, they needed to know how to keep themselves safe. Truly, that was an easy platform for Al and me. The difficult part was offering myself as an example of what not to do. I had to take an honest, long look at my own sex life to assess how I wound up where I was.

So I wrote, "As a teenager in high school, I didn't date much. I was so busy in shows or rehearsals. To tell you the truth, I was actually kind of shy about guys. Most of my socializing was done in groups. After high school, I attended the University of Miami in Florida. While I was there I had an experience with a young man that, until recently, I just called a 'really bad date.' Years later, after counseling, I learned that it was an oral sex date rape of a naïve 20-year-old. By the time I was 21, I decided to lose my virginity, so I called a guy I knew from high school that I considered a good friend."

I wondered how he was and what he was doing. I was always crazy about this guy, but he treated me more like a sister than a girlfriend. Several years later I found out the reason why.

I continued to write, "In retrospect, I realize that the overriding force that shaped the way I handled my sexual relationships was that bad experience at the University of Miami. I had developed a fear and my fear kept me silent. It was easier for me to get on the pill than it was to talk to my partner about protection. The fear of speaking up for myself was very powerful. It froze my mind, my heart and my soul. It led me down a very dangerous path. I wish I had a dollar for every time I have said or thought, if only I'd..." If only I had told Mom or Marie about that bad date. If only I'd insisted on the "no glove no love" rule EVERY time. If only I'd carried a condom and wasn't too shy to give it to the guy or put it on him myself...If only I'd....

During my senior year in college I fell madly in love with Patrick. When Patrick told me that he was gay, I was crushed. We never slept together, which made me question myself. "What's wrong with me? Why am I drawn to sensitive, gay men?" I questioned my sexuality. "Why did I feel so sexually inept?" Marie told me that she had slept with a lot of guys, but all I could think of was, why hadn't I? I watched the soap operas on TV and longed for a powerful, romantic sexual experience like the ones portrayed on my favorite *soap operas. I wanted an experience with a guy just one time with no strings attached.*

Shortly after I moved to New York, I decided to find a real "man," some sexy hunk of a guy, and maybe have a one-night stand with him. That guy turned out to be lethal "Ethan"(not his real name). We met in the Lincoln Center Library. He was a law student at N.Y.U. On our first date I slept with him. He didn't use a condom but I was on the pill and he pulled out, so I figured that I was safe. I was so appalled by my own behavior that every time Ethan called me afterwards for a date, I turned him down. I just couldn't face him. I felt that all he wanted was to sleep with me and that was not who I was. So I buzzed him off. Finally after a few months, he stopped calling and I was so relieved.

The irony of all of this is that the first man I could ever discuss protection and HIV with was Al. Before Al, if the guy wouldn't use a condom, I just couldn't tell him to do it. I later learned that many women felt the same way that I did. Many of them shared their stories with me of unhappy sexual experiences and/or not being able to communicate with their partners for fear of ruining the relationship, etc.

Dee Dee told me her sexual history before she ever went public with it. We were close, but it was her style to share her experiences with me after-the-fact. However she never shared with me the incident that happened at the University of Miami. Dee Dee was depressed during the first half of her sophomore year at Miami, but I had no idea what had happened or when. Only when she prepared to go public about her AIDS did I learn about the incident that happened around the beginning of her sophomore year. She had just returned to school after spending six weeks touring the Soviet Union in a production of *Peace Child.*

"Hi, Mom. It's me. I'm back in New York. The plane leaves for Miami in a few minutes but I just had to let you know how fabulous *Peace Child* was."

Dee Dee had been blown away by her experience performing with Soviet children for the Politburo on the

Black Sea. It was the climax of a six-week tour of the Soviet Union, which began in Moscow during the summer of 1988. The musical theater show was a plea for peace and the elimination of nuclear weapons of destruction. The cast was made up entirely of children—American and Soviet children. The show made a powerful statement about peace. Dee Dee was 19, older than most, when she did the tour. It was the summer between her freshman and sophomore year at college. Her breathtaking call from the airport said it all. "Mom, I've never felt this way before. It was so special using my talent for such a great purpose. By the way, I only have a dollar in my pocket, which is why I'm calling collect. And, Mom, I gave almost all of my clothes to the Soviet kids!"

"Dee Dee, are you telling me you returned home with only the clothes you are wearing and no money?"

"Yeah, pretty much, Mom. Oh, but I have some wonderful medals and trinkets given to me by my Soviet friends. Mom, they wanted my jeans and sneakers so I gave them those things. We can always buy more. Oops, that's my flight. I'll call you when I get to Miami. Love you. Bye."

With that she was off. Dee Dee was obviously electrified by her tour. When she called me from Kennedy Airport, I just wanted to hear her voice and know that she was safely back on American soil. We had been totally incommunicado during the six weeks she was on tour and I was very relieved to talk to her. She flew directly back to school.

When she called from Miami a few weeks later and sounded unhappy, I could not say that I was surprised. If anything, I felt exasperated. I tried to tell her before she decided to do *Peace Child* that the start of her fall semester would not give her any time in Dallas to unwind and share her experiences with me and others before returning to school. She assured me it would not matter. Right.

At first Dee Dee complained that the kids at school were shallow and materialistic. I thought it must be hard for her to shift gears from the depths of her emotional summer tour to the school theater department. She groused about the egotistical actors in her department. The Soviet and Marxist trinkets that she had collected on her trip were displayed on her bulletin board in her room. Her Cuban friends were not too pleased with her so-called communist leanings. Dee Dee needed to talk about *Peace Child* but not many people were interested in listening to her.

I just assumed she was having a reentry problem. Inexplicably, as the semester wore on, she just got sadder and sadder. Worried and fearing she was seriously depressed, in November I suggested that perhaps she should withdraw from school and return home to Dallas.

Dee Dee did not want to quit school. Quitting anything was not something she did very easily. She had a lifetime of persisting against the odds, so she hung in there.

Finally, she decided. "Mom, I'm going to return home after I finish this semester. I think I'll go to a local junior college and change my major. I'm sick of theater classes."

This was not my Dee Dee. Was I concerned when she moved back home? Sure I was but she was not very happy in her freshman year either. When she returned home midsophomore year, I did not query her any further because she had stopped crying after she had made the decision to return home. Once home, she did not hole up in her room and her eating pattern appeared normal so I figured that whatever was depressing her in Miami was over.

Dee Dee registered for several liberal arts classes at Brookhaven Junior College and even found a job teaching a lighting class at her high school. When the owner of the Dallas Children's Theater, Robyn Flatt, learned that she was back in Dallas, Robyn called her to request that she audition for several of their spring productions. A requested audition is almost a sure putt to a role and that is pretty much how it worked out. Dee Dee's interest in theater was rekindled through performance. Her attitude toward theater work steadily improved.

I never had a clue about that bad date in Miami. It was not until Dee Dee read me her statement that I learned about her date rape and, all of a sudden, the pieces fell into place. Do I regret that she did not see a counselor after she returned to Dallas? Of course I do. Would she have gone for counseling had I encouraged her to do it? I will never know. But if she had spoken to someone, anyone, about her experience in Miami, it might have made a difference in her behavior and life. As a mom trying to respect my daughter's privacy as she rocked and rolled her way through the breaking away years, perhaps this was one of those times that I should have found a way to invade her space. Maybe enlisting the help of a good friend, like Marie, might have helped. I will just never know.

Shortly after deciding that I would go public with my story I told Al, "I want to return to my synagogue, high school and college in Texas to talk to those kids."

"We will, Dee Dee. But, hey, let's get married first," Al replied. We laughed. Yes, in the midst of all of this craziness we were planning our wedding. Why? Because we wanted to be like any other couple in love, we wanted to make a commitment to one another.

Chapter Nine

UNENDING LOVE
November 1993-March 1994

November 4, 1993

AIDS or no AIDS, I'm still a young woman of 25 planning to be married. At first I wanted a small, simple but elegant traditional wedding. What I didn't want was to put the plans in place as early as Mom wanted me to do it. I gave her a hard time. So much was happening to me so fast. In my original life plan, I wasn't even going to get married until I was at least 30. By setting the date for March '94, I thought I wouldn't have to think about it for awhile. But Mom kept prodding me to get certain things done six months in advance! In my typical fashion, I dragged my feet. Mom stood her ground. As it turned out, she was right. I started to get really excited about the wedding when I opened the boxes of invitations we had selected. Al had scripted the wording and we jointly selected an unusual invitation with a piano and lovebirds colored lightly as if done with watercolors.

Al penned the following words, "A spark...A love...A challenge...A commitment brings Dee Dee Fields and Al McKittrick to cordially invite you to share in the joy and celebration of their wedding...."

Mom was wonderful about my wild wedding ideas. I told her I wanted a purple and green wedding. She didn't even balk at that. Every time I called her to add another name to our ever-expanding guest list, she never com-

plained. My idea of a small reception grew, like Topsy, to 168 guests. It's hard to believe that it is November and we have most of the plans for the wedding in place except for my dress and the flowers, which Al wants to do.

At first I told Mom I wanted a theatrical costume maker to sew me a dress. But I haven't gotten around to doing anything about it and Mom is getting nervous. So when she comes in for Thanksgiving, I think we'll look in the Cherry Creek Mall for a dress. I don't want a typical wedding gown. They're too expensive and a waste of money.

November 30, 1993

Mom and I were lucky to find a dress for the wedding in the Laura Ashley store in the Mall. It was a typical Laura Ashley dress of that time—informal, no train, simple but elegant. The top was scoop neck with gathered shoulders and long sleeves, all in lace over an illusion of a strapless gown form-fitted on top to a slightly flared cotton floor-length skirt. The dress was perfect for our Sunday afternoon wedding. It was just what I wanted and it was on sale for $400, which was considered inexpensive for a wedding dress. Mom and I were both pleased when the sample dress fit me like it had been made just for me, so we purchased it.

Many of my friends have planned weddings with their daughters. When they complain because they cannot find the perfect dress or veil or florist, I cringe and think, try planning a wedding with a daughter with the threat of death hanging over her head.

To make everything more tense, Dee Dee's health was deteriorating. Dr. Judy decided to take Dee Dee off AZT for awhile. She hoped that by giving Dee Dee's body a drug holiday, which is a brief time off drugs to cleanse the body, that her weight would stabilize and her anemia would improve. This was both a good and bad decision. The good news was her blood counts did improve and her weight stabilized, but by the time the wedding arrived, Dee Dee virtually had no immune system left.

As if we were not under enough stress with my daughter's health challenges, Marie, her maid-of-honor, called to tell us that she had cancer. (We later learned that Marie believed that she had cancer, but it was not true.) It was incredible—the bride had AIDS, the groom was HIV positive and now the maid-of-honor had cancer. The drama kicked into high gear as if any of us wanted or needed any more drama in our lives!

Our year closed with Howard's mother, Anna, dying on New Year's Eve. She was elderly and was living in a nursing home in Dallas for the past seven years. Alzheimer's Disease had robbed her of her personality long ago. Because, in a figurative sense, the Anna we knew had died years before, I thought her passing would be a blessing in disguise. But Howard and I were more affected by her death than we thought we would be. We were already in the grief process with our daughter. Anna's death brought home the finality of death and dying.

It was February 6, 1994. The wedding was one month away. I worried so much about Howard. He was very sad and distracted since his mother had died. I worried about Marie, too, who was suffering through her cancer treatments (so we believed). Would Marie be Dee Dee's maid of honor? My daughter would be heartbroken if Marie was too sick to come to the wedding.

I worried about Dee Dee and Al. They were busy doing all this wedding stuff. They both seemed nervous and overwhelmed by the amount of time, money, and planning it was taking to pull off the wedding of Dee Dee's dreams. My daughter was determined not to be sick at her wedding. She never knew how she was going to feel on any given day when she woke up. She could not control this part of her life. Why oh why hadn't I convinced her to do a small family wedding? Maybe I would not feel this way next month, but where was my sanity in all of this? "Oh, God, I just want to give Dee Dee her day as a real Cinderella—do not let HIV steal the wedding of her dreams."

It was 3 a.m. I was up again because everything was running through my mind. Would Al be a good husband for Dee Dee? After all, he had three ex-wives. And, how do two people with HIV get through a marriage? Our family dog had almost died the previous day. He rallied but it was only a matter of time before I would have to put him to sleep. "Why God?" I begged. "Why are you testing me?"

Those wee hours of the morning were some of my bleakest moments. Many nights I would fall asleep in Howard's arms crying. He worried about me and I worried about him. I read somewhere that worrying was like sitting in a rocking chair. You go nowhere. Believe me, worrying is wasted energy. I wanted to be brave like Dee Dee. She told me she was afraid to start crying because she feared that she would never be able to stop. I felt like Humpty-Dumpty before the fall, and feared that, if I fell apart, nobody would be able to put me back together again. In my private moments I cried. I talked to God a lot, too. And, as the wedding approached, I asked God to let my daughter live to have her day and to celebrate her first wedding anniversary.

February 28, 1994

Marie arrived in Denver last night. It's only one week till the wedding. She said that she wanted to help me get ready. The problem is, she's sick, too. Now poor Al has two sick girls on his hands. Marie told us that she's been throwing up blood. I'm so worried about her. She brought a wig with her to wear for the wedding since she was bald from the chemo. We're quite a pair. To me she looks beautiful. We're truly sisters. This was a special girl-time for us. Everything was going to be grand in spite of it all.

March 1, 1994

Yesterday Marie and I went shopping in the mall. We were in a store looking for a special nightie for my wedding night. All of a sudden everything just went black. The next thing I knew a pair of medics were taking me to Denver General. They told me that I had a seizure and had fallen in the store. I hit the tile floor pretty hard and possibly had a mild concussion. Al met us at the hospital. He looked very frightened.

The doctors ran a series of tests and immediately started me on Dilantin, an anti-seizure medication. I am not sure if it's the medication or the concussion but I'm so sleepy. Al's so sweet. I was scared about being in the hospital last night, so he stayed with me. That was my first time actually being admitted into the hospital. I've been through a lot of procedures, treatments, blood tests and blood transfusions, but all of those were done as an outpatient in the I.D. clinic.

Al called my folks. He turned white as he made the call. He had that same look on his face the day he called my parents from the hospital in Lima, Ohio. Daddy answered the phone. Luckily Mom was at her chorale retreat. Dad stayed pretty cool. The doctors only wanted to keep me in the hospital overnight for observation.

I'm being released from the hospital a little later. The doctors can't find the cause of my seizure so they're saying it's an HIV-related seizure. Whenever I have something that the docs can't explain, it automatically becomes an HIV-related thing. Personally, I really don't care. I just want to go home to my own bed.

I don't know why but Marie is angry with Al for not paying more attention to her problems. Poor guy. I don't think he knows whom to help first. We surely didn't need this to be happening to us just days before the wedding.

When I returned home from my chorale retreat, I got the news. Fortunately, Dee Dee was already back home from the hospital. I talked to her and tried to remain calm. I was scheduled to fly to Denver for the wedding the next day and told Howard we should not cancel the wedding, at least not until I could assess the situation. Howard agreed with me. "Dee Dee's never missed a performance and I doubt that she'll miss her own wedding."

After I saw her, I was not so sure. Dee Dee became more alert with each passing day. But, if the truth were known, until the day of the wedding, I would not have promised you a bride.

The next evening Howard and I took everyone out for dinner. Both of the girls spent more time in the bathroom than at the table and, believe me, they were not in there primping themselves.

Our out-of-town guests started to arrive on Friday for the Sunday wedding. To add to the normal tension of having people traveling to Denver in March with the hint of snow in the forecast, we had Dee Dee's newest health crisis to deal with. The bride stayed home to rest. I did not tell the guests the whole story. I did not want to worry everyone.

On Saturday evening Dee Dee came to the rehearsal and dinner party. She was still pretty tired. We had two ministers, one to do a metaphysical ceremony and one to do the Jewish traditions. We begged them both to keep the ceremony short because the bride and maid-of-honor were so sick. I do not think either of them heard us. After the rehearsal, Dee Dee went upstairs to our hotel room to rest before the dinner party.

Did Dee Dee make the wedding on Sunday? What do you think? The show must go on. Dee Dee was the consummate actress. She hit her mark! The love and intensity in the eyes of the bride and groom as they took their vows under the wedding canopy was breathtaking. The wedding was a beautiful blending of Jewish traditions and the metaphysical doctrines of the Unity church. Al had written the processional music inspired by his love for his bride. According to Jewish tradition, Howard and I walked our daughter down the aisle. After we gave her to her future husband, we proceeded to the wedding canopy. When Al gently took Dee Dee from our arms, I just knew that he was the right man for our daughter.

Pale as Dee Dee was, she simply glowed as any healthy bride would. From the top of her upswept hairdo which was meticulously designed and created by Greg (a dear friend who later died from AIDS), to the beautiful gown that bedazzled her frail body, she was Cinderella transformed for the ball. Dee Dee was genuinely happy and it warmed my heart. I glanced at the gathering of so many friends and family members who traveled from near and far to witness the wedding. I was proud of them and honored by their presence.

As the ceremony stretched on I worried whether my daughter would hold up. I was so nervous for her during the ceremony I could barely pay attention to the ministers' words. The ceremony concluded with the breaking of the glass and everyone yelled "Mazel Tov!" I finally relaxed. Al took his bride and lifted her gently off the floor into his arms and gave her a delicate kiss.

And the partying began. Everyone knew the bride had AIDS and the groom was HIV positive, but today she was a bride and he was her bridegroom and nothing else mattered. There was music and laughter and love. So many people told us that they were having a wonderful time. Dee Dee giggled like a teenager when she teased the single women, pretending to throw her bouquet to them and then holding it once before tossing it in the air to them. She danced with her Daddy and I danced with Al. And they danced together, overshadowing the cloud of death. I was so proud of them.

Al and Dee Dee fed each other the first bites of their wedding cake and then Al took a napkin and gently wiped her hands as if he were handling a Dresden doll. Toward the end of the afternoon, when the song *That's What Friends Are For* played, a huge ring of people encircled the couple as they danced. Hugs, kisses and love flowed. I am so grateful to God for giving Dee Dee her wedding day unmarred by the horrors of HIV.

Marie's poem, "Maid-of-Honor," captures the essence of how we all felt that day.

I'll never forget the glorious day my best friend walked down the aisle,

I'll never forget the pearls on her dress, as sparkly as her smile.

I'll never forget how I hugged her tight, How we giggled from ear to ear;

I was holding on to my precious one, Who was holding life so dear.

I'll never forget my reeling thoughts, As I stood next to her

How "love is rare and life is strange," And nothing is for sure.

I'll never forget the look on her face, How we all held our breath as they said, "I do"—

How the bitter sweetness lingered.

I'll never forget how he twirled her round when they danced as man and wife,

How lilting was his ladylove, Though labored was her life.

Dee Dee and Al's wedding was a testament to life—to wrap your arms around every single minute of it every day you are given!

March 8, 1994

I know that I gave everyone quite a scare the week before my wedding. Believe me, no one was more frightened than I was. I had never had a seizure before and I didn't like yet another thing about my body that I couldn't control. Damn that HIV! I'm so exasperated. If it hadn't been for Marie and Al's help, I don't think I'd have ever have made it down the aisle on my wedding day. Thank goodness Mom had pushed us to have all our plans in place early.

My wedding day was just perfect. I believe that God carried me that day. Marie was great. She helped me dress. She even remembered to bring a beautiful pair of pearl ear-

rings for me to wear. She gave me a special charm bracelet filled with pictures of all the people that I love.

The ceremony was a bit longer than I had hoped it would be, but it was beautiful. Al and I used the time to drink in each other with our eyes. I know that Mom was very worried about me, but she tried not to do her mother-hover thing for which I was so grateful. The most meaningful part of the reception was the huge circle of people who engulfed us as we danced to That's What Friends Are For. *I felt enveloped in God's love and very deeply connected to everyone who was there that special day. Al had a hansom horse-drawn carriage waiting for us. We changed our clothes and took our exit. Snow was falling from the sky as I climbed into the carriage. Al pulled a thick blanket into my lap and we waved goodbye. I felt like Cinderella leaving the ball with her Prince Charming to live happily ever after.*

Dee Dee
Age 23
New York
July 1992

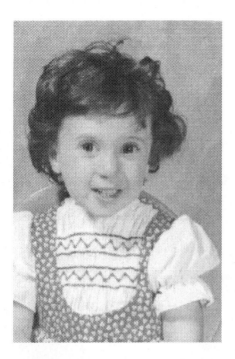

Dee Dee
Age 3
1971

Dee Dee's Bat Mitzvah Party
Age 13
September 1982

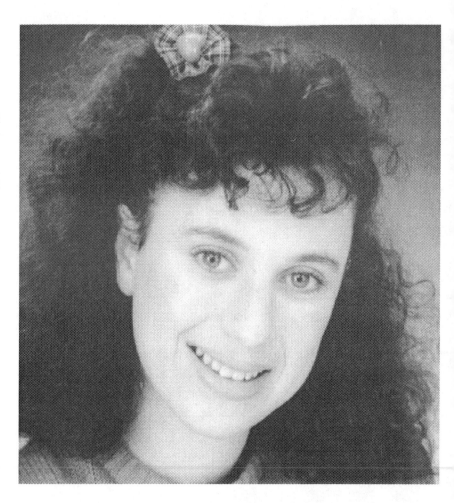

Dee Dee
Age 18
1986

Dee Dee with Mom
Cinderella Tour
Tyler, Texas
February 1993

Dee Dee and Al
Married
March 6, 1994

Photograph © Gerald Shuster

Dee Dee and Al
Wedding Dance
March 6, 1994
Photograph © Gerald Shuster

Chapter Ten

HAPPILY EVER AFTER
Spring 1994

March 9, 1994

We spent our wedding night at a bed-and-breakfast in Denver. It was deliciously romantic. The next day we left for our honeymoon in Hawaii.

I just cannot believe my parents. They hosted the rehearsal dinner and my magnificent wedding and even gave us this wonderful honeymoon on Maui. I'll write Mom a long thank you note when we return home. I'm truly a blessed little girl. So many parents have deserted their adult children with HIV. I'm so lucky to have Mom and Dad's unconditional love. Sometimes I feel guilty because I can't give them grandchildren. Thank God my brother and Denise gave them a grandson. Al has helped me work through so many of my guilt feelings. I never would have made it to this day without his devotion, love and wacky wonderful sense of humor.

Hawaii is just beautiful. Al and I are having a great time in spite of the rainy weather. I suffered another seizure yesterday and spent a short time in the Maui Hospital. It wasn't on our itinerary. But hey, when you're dealing with HIV, things just happen which aren't part of the plan. Either I go with the flow or end up in a black pit having a pity party. Not for me.

March 15, 1994

I saw Dr. Judy today and she adjusted my Dilantin level after I told her about the seizure in Hawaii. I feel so drugged. The medicine has changed my bouncy personality into someone who is quiet and low-key. I'm not sure my mood is all drug-induced. I'm very frightened. And to make matters worse, now my driving privileges are suspended for at least a year and if I am not seizure-free, I can't get the restriction removed. Oh God, why me?

Marie called last night and told us that she had tested positive for TB when she returned to New York (another fabrication we later learned). At first we worried that she had the drug-resistant strain of TB but thank goodness, it was the treatable variation. Al and I told Dr. Judy about Marie and the TB. She insisted that we add the drug INH to our regimen as a precautionary measure. Al has to do a three-month course of it but, lucky me, I have to do it for a year. Dr. Judy asked me to be patient while she adjusted my drug levels. She also started me on a new HIV drug called D4T (Zerit). My body feels like it's on chemical overload, but I have no choice. I wish I had more confidence in the HIV drugs. What I didn't know then is that D4T would give me my best year followed by my worst one ever.

When I complained to Mom about not being able to drive, she devised a cute plan that she thought would solve the problem. She then suggested that we hire a "driving Miss Dee Dee" à la driving Miss Daisy, which she offered to pay for. At first I got pissed at her and said, "No way." I am sure my anger was tied to my frustration with the loss of my independence. And I just hated for my folks to have another HIV-related expense. The new car was enough.

A few months later I relented. We hired Shawn Marie, a young woman and an out-of-work actress. She was around my age. Al referred to her as our "personal assistant." Believe it or not, after awhile, I liked it when she drove me to do an errand or to an appointment. It helped me feel less dependent on Al. And, in time, I didn't miss driving a car at all.

April 4, 1994

Everything is happening so fast. I got that fatal blood test result. You now have zero T-cells! None, zip, nada. I'm so scared. I know everyone else is worried, too. How much longer can I live with no T-cells before I get one of those nasty OIs? Every moment of every day feels even more tenuous. I feel myself spinning down deeper in a hole.

April 15, 1994

Mom called and asked me to travel to Miami for a bat mitzvah with her and Dad next month. I said, "Sure." I've decided to grab every opportunity to do something fun. Even though I know that Al's schedule won't allow him to make the trip with me in May, I want to see my family in Miami. Maybe I have to prove to myself that I can travel without Al.

May 5, 1994

I returned to Denver from Miami last night. I'm not sure if it was the separation from Al or just how I was feeling but I was compelled to talk to him about the things I wanted to do before I died. I never quite put it in so many words, because I didn't believe that I was near the end of my life but I knew my situation was becoming very grave. I needed some goals...some things I wanted to experience for myself and with Al. I wanted to own my own home, to swim with the dolphins and to return to Texas to speak at my synagogue, high school and college. I was determined to squeeze as much living into each good day I was given. Al convinced me to do our talks in Texas in the fall. We thought it might be fun to plan to swim with the dolphins in Florida next January when it would be cold and nasty in Denver.

Buying a house became the first item on our agenda. The house we were renting had our master bedroom upstairs and the stairs were getting increasingly more difficult for me to climb. On the days that I didn't feel well, I felt trapped in our bedroom upstairs. If I needed a drink from the kitchen, Al had to run up the stairs to give it to me. We even purchased baby monitors so Al could hear me when I called him. It wasn't the best solution, but it did help. (The baby monitors were another one of Mom's suggestions, one she learned from her support group.) We needed to get our bedroom on the main floor and have a convenient space for Al's studio where he taught his voice and piano students.

I presented the house idea to Mom and Dad. After all, we couldn't afford to buy a house on our own. I hoped after I was gone, Al could have a place to live for a while, or the house could become a home for people living with HIV. I needed Mom and Dad's financial help. I still have a little money saved from tour but my folks would have to sign on the mortgage and come up with almost all of the down pay-ment. We'd make the monthly mortgage payments. It sounded like a fair arrangement and lucky for me, the folks supported the plan. I guess they wanted to help me realize part of the American dream—to own my own home.

Al and I loved house hunting. We were excited when we found this adorable restored Victorian house in a much better neighborhood just a seven-minute drive north of downtown Denver. We purchased the house in June and moved into our wonderful new-old home shortly thereafter.

Following the wedding, Dee Dee had more than her share of increasing health challenges but, in spite of it all, she was happy.

"Mom, I know this may sound crazy, but I *am* happy. I love my life with Al. And I love the work I'm doing—speaking to groups about HIV/AIDS. It gives me so much satisfaction. I feel like I'm finally doing something rewarding with my talent, like I felt when I had performed in the Soviet Union with *Peace Child.*"

I believe the life Dee Dee shared with Al was a happy one. They met the challenge of living with AIDS…the blood tests, the transfusions, the rashes, the fe-vers, the constant testing and prodding, the pills, the fa-tigue…with a grace that defies explanation. Like so many parents, it was music to my ears to hear my child say that she was happy. Some adult-children do not ever experience the kind of success and happiness Dee Dee did. In the middle of this firestorm there were many blessed moments, hard as that may be to believe.

In June, Howard and I traveled to Denver to complete the purchase of their house. She and Al had found the perfect home for them. It was a restored two-story Victorian house with complete living quarters on the first floor. The living room was a small parlor with a fireplace and opened into the dining room that was about twice the size of the living room. The kitchen was modernized and big enough to hold a small table and chairs. The washing machine and dryer were conveniently located behind double doors in the kitchen. Behind the kitchen was a room, which Dee Dee visualized for her craft/sewing room as well as a place for their futon and a desk. The master bedroom was off the dining room, as was the main bathroom, all very convenient for Dee Dee. Upstairs was a loft space for Al's piano and synthesizer, a bathroom and another bedroom that would make an ideal "in-law suite." A small deck could be accessed from the loft onto the roof. In this house my daughter would never have to climb the stairs if she chose not to.

The house was located in a better neighborhood and was in much better condition than the house that they were renting. I was happy for the two of them as I remembered how thrilled we were when we purchased our first home. It might not have been practical for Howard and me to own a second home in Colorado just then, but it gave us great joy to help our daughter live more comfortably for however long that would be. Dee Dee wanted a backyard swing and a vegetable garden. Al set up a back yard swing and planted a garden and with a friend built a deck on the back of the house. No request from Dee Dee was too much for Al.

Before we knew about the house, Paul Simon, the composer-entertainer, had announced that he would be giving an AIDS benefit concert in Dallas at the end of June. We had purchased four tickets and planned to fly Dee Dee and Al to Dallas to attend the concert. They were both enthralled. Following the concert, we invited some of our friends over for dinner and a visit with Dee Dee and Al. I had a cake to celebrate Al's birthday.

Dee Dee and Al entertained us with mirth and song, only this concert was much shorter than they had done for us before. It was a great weekend, another happy memory.

I needed that fun weekend. It had been a rough spring for me personally. In addition to living through the joy and trauma of the wedding, I was in a minor car accident in May and aggravated an old neck injury. I was doing physical therapy again. Then our family dog took a turn for the worst and we had to put him to sleep.

During that time, a dear friend said, "Life should go smoothly for you. You have enough just to deal with your daughter."

In reality, life does not happen that way. There were days when it was very hard for me to keep my focus on the half-*full* cup rather than the half-*empty* part. On those days I must have read the serenity prayer 50 times. I was living the calamity of my daughter's illness and it felt as if other events were conspiring, at times, to tow me under. Where are you God? Give me the strength I need for this journey.

One of the sources of my strength, I know, came from my grandson, Ben. I tried to conclude each trip to Denver with a visit with him. He renewed my faith in life. Ben's hugs and kisses and innocence were the best medicine ever. Grandchildren are the delicious desserts of life.

Chapter Eleven

AIDS 101
Fall 1994

Sitting in the audience watching Dee Dee and Al give their AIDS 101 presentation was a privilege and a thrill. They were a dynamic duo but it was Dee Dee who mesmerized her audience.

The first time I saw them do their number was in Denver. They were invited to speak in a HUD housing project populated with elderly residents. When AIDS patients were approved for residency, the seniors were afraid that they were going to "catch" AIDS from using the same utensils, dishes and cups, drinking fountains and toilets as the AIDS residents, even though this was just not true.

Dee Dee and Al gave their HIV 101, a basic explanation of HIV/AIDS, which included how it was contracted. My daughter told the audience that she could identify with them. "Even though I may look young," she said, "there are many days when I feel old because I have so many aches and pains." It was an immediate equalizer as she bridged the gap to this senior group.

At the end of the presentation Dee Dee and Al fielded many questions. Most of the people were worried about blood transfusions they received after surgeries in the 1980s and early 1990s. Dee Dee reassured them that the blood supply after 1986 had been screened and could be considered safe. But she was always an advocate for testing and reminded her audience that the only way to know your status for sure was to get tested for HIV, a test that was then and still is today only given upon your request. Though my daughter spoke to many different adult groups including caregivers such as hospice and health care providers, her favorite audiences were young people.

She usually opened her segment, or closed it depending on the circumstances, with the song *Hero*. *There's a hero, if you look inside your heart...you don't have to be afraid of what you are...*She boldly told her story—never pulling any punches...*There's an answer if you reach into your soul...*She answered any and every question she was asked if she knew the answer....*And the sorrow that you know will melt away...*And if she did not know the answer, she would find the answer later and call the person who had posed the question...*Then a hero comes along with the strength to carry on...and you cast your fears aside and you know you can survive....* At first, I thought Dee Dee sang *Hero* to Al. Now I wonder if she chose that song for her presentations after Pat Schroeder said she was a hero to other women. Personally, I believe she was sending a message to her audiences, affirming each person's individual strength to be his or her *own* hero.

Dee Dee never allowed any videotaping or recording of her presentations because she wanted to protect her audiences' anonymity. She also felt that a camera or other equipment would inhibit people from asking questions. She distributed three by five note cards before her presentation began, especially to her young audiences so they could write their questions on a card if they did not feel comfortable asking them in a group.... *So, when you feel like hope is gone, look inside you and be strong and you'll finally see the truth that a hero lies in you.*

It was all about the audience with Dee Dee, whether she was on a stage to entertain or in front of a group to educate about AIDS. And the lyrics of the song she sung had to say it all. She was a unique performer who came to believe her God-given talent was supposed to be used for this greater purpose.

In August, just a few weeks before the Colorado AIDS Walk, Dee Dee contracted a nasty eye infection. We all feared that it was CMV, the virus that caused blindness in AIDS patients. When she tested negative for CMV, we all breathed a collective sigh of relief. The eye infection turned out to be the result of an adverse drug reaction.

One week later, Dee Dee called to tell me she needed another blood transfusion. She sounded discouraged. Her low blood counts resulted in a huge lack of energy and it was causing her to lose her will to fight. I reminded her how energized she felt after her last transfusion.

The Walk, however, invigorated her more than any added blood cells. I witnessed the rekindling of her fighting spirit. She had taken many hits over the past year and suffered many losses since she had been diagnosed with AIDS, but she refused to dwell on the losses. Her spirit prevailed. It was hard to feel sad around her because her personality was so upbeat most of the time.

In September of '94, Dee Dee and Al were made honorary chairmen for the Colorado AIDS Walk. They spoke briefly and sang *Somewhere Over the Rainbow* again, this time to inspire the crowd of 10,000 walkers. Then my daughter pledged to be at AIDS Walk '95 if everyone there would do the same. It was quite a commitment for her to make considering her T-cells were nonexistent and her health so fragile, but her will was strong. The crowd responded to her with thunderous applause; it was one of those special moments in time. If she made the promise to be there next year then somehow, some way, she would keep that promise.

October 1, 1994

Mom and Dad always wanted me to participate in a clinical trial or to do some cutting edge HIV treatment but I was afraid to be a guinea pig. Everything I read excluded women in the preliminary studies. I had this sense that drugs designed for men may not be so good for me. I was darn stubborn about this because it was one of those few areas left in my life left that I could control. I know my folks were ecstatic when, following the Walk, I agreed to see a renowned AIDS researcher in Denver. At that time I was doing pretty well on D4T so when I saw him he didn't suggest that I do anything differently. He was familiar with my case since all the HIV cases in Denver were followed closely by a team of doctors that included the clinical ones that I saw in D.G. and the research doctors. It was pretty much learn as you go for all of them, but somehow it gave me comfort to know that they all reviewed my case. Life had changed for me in so many ways, but I was determined to meet the challenge.

Dee Dee planned to return to Dallas in November to speak at her high school and at our synagogue. Ever since she was a little girl, her Jewish heritage played an important role in her life. She was three years old when we moved from Cherry Hill, New Jersey to Dallas, Texas. We enrolled her in a Jewish Sunday school in Cherry Hill and then in one in Dallas. She looked forward to attending each Sunday and appeared to be enjoying the experience.

A few years later, Howard and I and five other couples in our community founded a conservative synagogue, Congregation Beth Torah. Twenty-five years later, it is a thriving congregation with over 400 member families. Some of my fondest memories are of Dee Dee sitting in the lap of our visiting rabbi during the first High Holiday Services. She especially loved holding and hearing a small ram's horn (shofar) blown during the services. To this day, the shofar's shrill sounds conjure up images of my baby girl.

Dee Dee led the new congregation in song when she was six years old. Performing in front of the congregation did not intimidate her in the least. Even today, the young children still lead the congregation in some of the prayers. In addition to singing, she also enjoyed the Jewish holidays and rituals with her favorite holiday being Passover.

November 5, 1994

At my core, I'm Jewish. While I was at college, I attended the Unity Church and a Catholic Church as part of a spiritual quest but I always came back to my Jewish roots. After that time I liked to refer to myself as a metaphysical Jew. Growing up I remember my brother rebelled against religion, but he rebelled at anything that was an organized group. Maybe I was drawn to Judaism because my brother wasn't. I told Mom and Dad that they were too religious for Alan. Mom made us get dressed up for services. I liked getting dressed up whereas Alan hated the stiffness. I looked forward to and enjoyed the unusual Passover foods at our Passover seders. Alan would squirm during the seder service and complain that all the Passover foods tasted the same to him. When it came to Hebrew school, though, Alan excelled and he did an outstanding job at his bar mitzvah. "Mr. Perfect," I used to call him since he always did well in every school setting. He was a hard act to follow.

Me, I liked learning the Hebrew language. It was easy for me because of my natural tendency to turn letters around and to read from right to left. I liked the kids I met at synagogue, too. When I was old enough I joined Kadima, our synagogue junior youth group. Guess I was just much more of a social butterfly than my brother. And, my interest in Judaism really pleased my parents.

My bat mitzvah was very special. The ceremony was very meaningful. What I remember the most, however, is that Mom had a special dress sewn for me. I was too tiny to find a sophisticated dress that fit. Unlike my friends whose parents planned every detail, I planned my own party following my bat mitzvah and gave it a Broadway theme. At 13, I had Broadway dreams! I made the centerpieces for the tables using top hats, canes, white gloves and sheet music from different shows. The place cards for the party were "tickets" to the show (or table). There was a huge sign on the wall of the reception room that read "Welcome to Broadway." We had a sign that looked like a marqee in the lobby area that read, "Diane's Bat Mitzvah Starring Diane Fields." (That was before I decided to use my nickname, Dee Dee, as my stage name.) The candle lighting ceremony was the high point of the party for me. After it ended, I stood on a chair with a microphone in hand and belted the song Tomorrow *from* Annie. *At 13, the Jewish community celebrated my becoming an adult, but for me it was my theatrical debut.*

All those memories came flooding back to me the moment that Al and I stepped inside my synagogue to speak to the kids on that Sunday morning in November. We met the group in the library. It was just the kids and Al and me...no teachers or rabbi. The children were ages 13 to 16 and were surprisingly open with us. (That day turned out to be one of the highlights of my AIDS journey.) Their questions suggested that some of them were sexually active already and not using protection. Some kids talked about their "friends" who were using drugs. It was a real eye-opener to me. I just never expected it from the kinds of kids I used to run with. I hoped that after our presentation, they wised up.

After addressing the young people, we gave a different presentation to the adults in the main sanctuary. About 125 people came to hear us talk—more people than anyone ever expected to come to hear an HIV/AIDS presentation. After the presentation, someone asked me if I questioned God after this happened to me. I told the audience that God had not given me AIDS. I never blamed God for my condition. I told them that misfortune randomly happened to people all the time, bad things that are unavoidable. However, this virus was avoidable.

November 1994

Before Al and I returned to Dallas to give our presentation on AIDS awareness at my high school, I wrote to Marie. "These were not the circumstances that I pictured for my return to Arts. I thought that I would some day return to Arts to give a talk on my Broadway career and to give the kids advice on how to make it in the biz."

Marie wrote back to me. "Do you have any idea how much of a difference you are making in those kids' lives? You are more than telling those kids how to be actors. You're modeling for them how to be 'live-ers.' You're center stage, in the spotlight, and you're saving their lives! Dee Dee, maybe you think that you are educating people about AIDS, but what you are also teaching them are real lessons in courage, spirit, passion and strength."

Marie sure had a way of setting me straight with her wit and wisdom. I wanted to touch people through theater. I never imagined it would be my life story that would touch people this way. Marie was my best cheerleader. Speaking at Arts triggered another amazing flood of memories.

On that same trip, Dee Dee returned to her alma mater, the Booker T. Washington High School for the Performing and Visual Arts, affectionately nicknamed Arts Magnet. The magnet schools were developed in Dallas during that time as a response to desegregation to integrate formerly all black high schools. Dee Dee's interest in acting germinated long before she attended high school. The acting bug bit her in elementary school in the fourth grade in *You're a Good Man Charlie Brown* when she played the role of the dog, Snoopy. She did not get to utter one word, but I could always tell what Snoopy was thinking by her movements.

School was pretty much a drag for me until my fourth grade teacher cast me in a play as Snoopy. I didn't have a speaking part but I got ideas how to act from watching our family dog, a Schnauzer named Novy. I remember asking Mom what Novy was thinking. She looked at me very strangely. Finally, the day of the show arrived. I got to wear a Snoopy costume. I just loved the audience laughter and the applause. I was hooked. At last, I could shine at something.

It is ironic that Charlie Brown was this lovable kid who never won a baseball game. In football, he doesn't get to kick the ball because Lucy pulls it away from him at the last second. But everyone cheers for Charlie. He is this hopelessly average, good-hearted kid, who picks himself up and brushes himself off after every disaster. He just never gives up that last stubborn glimmer of hope. In so many ways, Dee Dee was our Charlie Brown.

After that play, Dee Dee wanted to be an actress. Her interest in Broadway musicals grew as she did. She told everyone that she wanted to be an actress when she grew up. Of course, that is what many little girls say. For that matter, most little girls are born actresses. Dee Dee begged me to take her to auditions. I was working and time was at a premium. I could not see myself in the role of a Mama Rose. I told her when she got older she could take herself to auditions. I did not think she was serious about acting until she and her girlfriend, Jennifer, auditioned for the Arts Magnet High School in downtown Dallas.

Jenny and I became best friends from the moment we met in the fourth grade. I had enrolled in this new school because my family had just moved to a new home in Far North Dallas in the middle of the school year. Jenny was this skinny, talkative little Jewish girl with brown curly hair. Most people thought we were twin sisters. We weren't in the same classroom, but our two classes were in one big space and were combined for many of our activities.

When we were 10-year-olds, Jenny and I just hung out at the Mall most of the time. One of the fun things we did was to visit the toy stores. We would ask the clerk to open the locked cases of expensive Steiff plush animals. We would play with them and then give them back to the clerk because they were too expensive for us to buy. We would giggle a lot and talk about what we wanted to be when we grew up. I, of course, wanted to be an actress on Broadway. Jenny, who drew beautifully, wanted to be an artist. She once drew a wonderful picture of my cat, Tuffy. I asked her to sign it for me because I wanted to say someday that I owned an original "Jennifer Roth." She laughed. I never doubted that we both would be successful. Jenny didn't believe in herself the way that I did. Well, to make a long story short, it was through Jennifer's mom that the two of us found our way to the Arts Magnet High School.

Dee Dee started her campaign to go to this special arts high school when she was in eighth grade. Jennifer's mom had the opportunity to take a tour of the facility through an art class. She just raved about it and she took Jennifer to see the school.

It started like an ordinary day in my life but it turned out to be a day that I'll never forget. As I sat in my classroom at Parkhill Junior High School preparing for another ho-hum day in eighth grade, Jennifer came running into the classroom all smiles and very excited.

"Dee Dee, I found it! It's great! You wouldn't believe it," she said, like a rapid-fire machine gun.

I could hardly understand what she was saying. When I calmed her down, she told me all about this fabulous school for the visual and performing arts in downtown Dallas.

For the next two weeks we talked non-stop about the possibility of going to the Arts Magnet High School. For Jenn, three hours of her school day would be art classes. I'd have three hours a day of theater classes. For both of us, there'd be three hours of regular studies in small classes with lots of personal attention. It sounded too good to be true. On the other hand, there were some drawbacks. We would not be able to be ninth graders in Parkhill Junior High because the new school was a four-year high school that started with ninth grade. The other two problems would be transportation and convincing our parents to pay a monthly tuition. One of my biggest concerns was that I'd have to audition to get accepted.

"Oh, Mommy, can I go to high school there, please, please, pretty please?" Dee Dee pleaded.

She would lobby her cause every chance that she got. I could not whip up too much enthusiasm for it. After all, the school was located downtown and we would have to pay tuition for her to attend. Dee Dee would be mixed with kids 14 to 18 years old. At 14, she barely looked 11. So I hoped that she would change her mind about this school. She changed her mind about other things fairly often. I acted neutral so as not to encourage or discourage her.

My parents tried not to influence my decision. My folks said if I decided to attend Arts, I needed to stick it out for at least one year. The decision was mine to make. It was not an easy one for me. I weighed all the pros and cons, but I still couldn't decide. Even though I didn't enjoy going to Parkhill, leaving my neighborhood school and all the kids I had known since elementary school was pretty scary. Even if Jenn and I would be going to the same school, once we were there, we'd be in different areas of studies called clusters. We probably wouldn't see much of each other during the school day. After lots of discussion and a tour of the school, Jenn and I decided that all of that didn't matter; we really wanted to go to Arts.

The first time I visited Arts, I fell in love with it. The atmosphere of the school was so different from my sterile junior high. I felt energy, an excitement in the air. It was obvious that the kids loved being there. I was greeted warmly by a teacher and given a tour by a senior in the theater department. I met several of the teachers in the theater department known as the theater cluster and they were so nice.

In my old junior high school there were many cliques. The jocks hung out with the jocks, the cheerleaders with other cheerleaders, the nerds with the nerds and the socials with the socials. Senior high school in my neighborhood would just be a repeat of that same scene. In Arts, the kids seemed different. They came from all different backgrounds and ages but were intertwined around an activity at lunchtime. I decided that this was a place that I could fit in. Why? Because to be different or an individual was to fit in at Arts. I set an appointment for my audition.

Dee Dee wanted to audition for Arts and she was one terrific salesperson. She just never let up. All year she campaigned. By May, I relented. I remember telling Howard, "It can't hurt to let her audition."

Howard gently reminded me, "If she gets accepted to that school, then you're the one who'll have to drive her back and forth to school every day."

"Yeah, but Dee Dee is our child who never wants to go to school and she's *begging* to go to this school." I took her to the audition.

I parked in the lot of this 100-year-old school building in the Dallas Arts District. I could not help but wonder why was Dee Dee drawn to this school? I did not have to wonder for very long. Having taught elementary school in my twenties, the teacher in me felt *it* from the moment I stepped into the building and walked down the corridors. I could feel the positive energy instantly. Kids were sitting everywhere, but they were not rowdy. Some were reading, some were sketching and others were practicing lines for plays. The kids were of every conceivable background and seemed genuinely excited to be there. All I could think was, "Martin Luther King and his dream was alive and well, right here in this school!" The atmosphere was magnetic. Finally, I could understand why Dee Dee was so attracted to the school.

Dee Dee led me down the corridor to the Experimental Theatre. The room was a little larger than a standard classroom with chairs for the parents and students, a stage at one end of the room, and a row of dirty windows on the wall perpendicular to the stage. Kids who had signed up to audition were just standing around. A panel of teachers who were the judges sat at a long table just inside of the doorway. Two of them recognized Dee Dee from her previous visit. Who did they assign number one for the audition process? They chose Dee Dee, but being first did not throw her at all.

When the process began, she got right up on the stage and performed whatever the judges asked her to do. First they asked her to skate across the stage on a cold wintry day. "In Dallas?" I thought to myself, "It is only 102 degrees outside. Who ice skates?" Dee Dee used her imagination and she did it well. One of the judges asked her to recite a monologue that she had previously prepared. She recited material from the *Diary of Anne Frank*. She related well to Anne Frank who, at 14, wrote her diary when she was hiding in an attic from Nazi soldiers during World War II.

I was a little nervous at my audition, but I knew that I could do it. My reading tutor had prepared me. We had worked together for three years on my dyslexia. She encouraged me to ask to review something new before I read it out loud. I hated for anyone to know that I had a reading problem and rarely asked for any special consideration.

Then Dee Dee was asked to do a "cold reading"…to read something that she had never seen before. She hesitated, then she bravely asked the judge to give her a few minutes to look it over. She never wanted to admit to anyone that she had learning disabilities, which made it difficult for her to read. Her reading tutor told Dee Dee to tell her teachers that she needed a little time to prepare before she could read aloud. On this day, she chose to tell the judges that she had dyslexia, quickly adding that she could do the reading with a little time to prepare. The judges responded by saying a reading would not be necessary. I know that she worried whether she had done the right thing.

When I told the judges about my learning disability, they just dismissed me. At first, I thought maybe I had blown it. If the audition wasn't hard enough, the days and weeks that followed were even more difficult. Jennifer got her acceptance letter first. I would run home from school every day and look for my letter, but nothing came. Finally, after I had almost given up hope, my acceptance letter arrived. God, was I thrilled! We posted that letter on our refrigerator where it stayed for months—the letter that changed the course of the rest of my life!

Chapter Twelve

LIFE AT ARTS
1983-1987

The careers of two skinny little Jewish girls from an upper middle-class neighborhood began when they boarded a school bus at a nearby Dallas high school to ride to school downtown. Dee Dee awoke early that morning...something unheard of from my night owl. She dressed quickly and was raring to go. She actually was looking forward to school.

August 17, 1983

My first day at Arts: I woke up before my alarm clock and was dressed for school before my brother, a major accomplishment. My parents were in shock when I came downstairs before him. I was ready for my day before anyone else. From that day, each and every day, I looked forward to going to school. That was an amazing transformation for me. It's hard to explain. I just felt at home from the moment that I entered the building at Arts. No one cared if I was short or tall, homely or cute, white or black, freshman or senior. What counted the most was my talent—first, last and always.

At 9 a.m. on the first day of school at the very first assembly, Miss Smith, our theater cluster coordinator gave the freshman theater class "The Talk." Her message was very straightforward and somewhat disheartening.

"Ninety-eight percent of all actors are unemployed," she began. *"Therefore you will learn many disciplines here. Your academic studies will always come first. Your classes will prepare you for college. Young people, our goal is not to just turn out actors but people who will understand and appreciate the arts, all aspects of it. Some of you will go on to become doctors, architects, lawyers and businesspeople. We hope when you graduate from this school that you will love and appreciate the arts. For those of you who choose to pursue a career in the performing arts, you'll leave here with much preparation, but that will not guarantee that you will become a working actor. Always have a Plan B. Keep your grades up and do not be absent from class before or during a show or you will NOT perform."*

Miss Smith was soft-spoken but very stern. She was setting the stage for our futures in a very tough business. I soon learned that this school was a training ground for future Dallas artists. It was hoped that someday we would return to the Dallas community and perform. The good news: Dallas Theater Center, Theater 3 *and* Dallas Children's Theater *always took a serious look at us when we auditioned for them. The directors knew "somehow" who we were and that we were serious about the business. The bad news: we did not automatically get cast into their productions. But we were in the network; we were connected and it helped.*

I remember how excited I was to get a minor role in a production of Cinderella *at the* Dallas Theater Center *when I was a sophomore. I was a character in the background with only a line or two, but it was a thrill to just appear on that stage. I also did* A Little Night Music *for* Theater 3. *However, the theater that became my second home was the* Dallas Children's Theater. *Doing children's theater was just perfect for me: I looked three years younger than my age, I had a lively personality, but most of all, I just loved playing to and being with kids.*

Dee Dee's freshman year at Arts was very challenging. She was cast in background minor roles. Her teachers underestimated her because of her small size. They assumed she was this princess from a privileged neighborhood who was not serious about acting or willing to work very hard. They were very demanding. If it had not been for Dee Dee's burning desire to become a professional actress and our pact, I am sure she would have resigned from the program more than once during her freshman year. When Dee Dee's teachers were hard on her, she would whine to me, "Why doesn't anyone ever take me seriously?" At those times, I tried to encourage her and I reminded her that she chose to go to this school. If it was too difficult, she could quit but she had agreed to give it at least one year.

My daughter sometimes sounded like Rodney Dangerfield complaining that she just did not get much respect. I believe it was because of her Sally Field-like appearance and her Gidget personality. I am not sure she ever put all that together. When she ran into situations like the one at Arts, she would just dig in her heels and become even more determined than ever to be successful. Somehow, she would prove to her teachers that she was serious.

As part of the freshman curriculum she was required to take a class on rejection. She was taught about the meaning of rejection. In the theater world, it was often less about the talent of an actor and more about how a director viewed the ensemble he wanted to cast. If a director did not cast an actor, it could be for the simple reason that he visualized a tall redhead in the role and you were a short brunette. It was a tough lesson for her to learn.

Dee Dee developed a director's eye as she looked for the roles that were her type. Her vivaciousness made her well-suited for character roles. Dee Dee often complained because she wanted to be the ingénue. After all, who does not want to be the star? Over time, she learned that the character roles were a lot more fun to play.

Her favorite class was musical theater, which was no surprise. The school only offered two years of musical theater, but Dee Dee was one of the first students to take it for three years. She remarked about the inferior status of the musical theater program in the school. It appeared not to be as respected as dramatic theater. Her teacher, Nedra, taught her to act out the lyrics of a song and encouraged her to audition in the community. "Serious actors think it is a lesser calling, but I love it," she once told me.

I was proud of Dee Dee. It took guts to walk into a totally new school setting even with Jennifer by her side. She and Jenn saw each other at the start of the school day but once classes began, their paths rarely ever crossed. In time, the two girls slowly drifted apart.

It took even more courage for Dee Dee to audition for shows in both the school and community and to learn to accept rejection. Knowing how difficult it is to be successful in show business, I had my doubts that she would become a professional performer. Regardless of the outcome, I became convinced that the Arts Magnet High School was a good environment for Dee Dee because her academic courses were integrated with her theater classes. Her creativity was stimulated constantly. She became motivated to learn and in time produced above average academic work. And, she loved it. How could I not be happy when she found a place to express and develop her passion?

My worries not only centered on academics and career opportunities for Dee Dee. The Arts Magnet was a melting pot of ethnic youth. I knew the dating scene could become a landmine. Before I allowed her to enroll at Arts, we discussed dating in general.

"Honey, I know the kids at Arts come from different backgrounds. It is important to me that you date your own kind," I began carefully.

"Mom, do you mean that I can't date a black guy?" She quickly shot back at me.

"I don't think it'd be a good idea. If you're all in a group say maybe after a show and everyone is going out for something to eat, I wouldn't consider that a date. But going out as a couple...."

"God, Mom, how bigoted can you be? Can I date someone who isn't Jewish?"

110

"Yeah, but it wouldn't be my preference," I reluctantly replied.

"Mom you're so narrow-minded!" my daughter exclaimed. She was angry with me for mentioning it even though she was not even interested in dating yet.

"Look, Dee Dee, that's my rule. Either you accept it or don't go to Arts." I felt very strongly about interracial dating and I let her know it.

She thought for a minute and then retorted, "Well, okay. I'll stay active in the B'nai Brith Girls while attending Arts." She agreed to remain a member of her Jewish youth group partly because she had friends in the group but also to placate me, because she desperately wanted to go to school at Arts.

Almost in the same breath she said "Mom?"

"Yes, Dee Dee."

"Were you a virgin when you married Dad?"

I looked at my 14-year-old who had just stomped her feet like a 10-year-old and was posing a question now like a 20-year-old.

Before I could answer her she second-guessed my answer and said, "Well, Mom, I don't plan to be. I plan to stay single for a long time. Maybe I'll get married when I'm 30. You were married when you were 21!"

I was not prepared to argue with her. I was relieved when the phone rang and cut short our discussion. For hours thereafter, I gave much thought to her statement. Dee Dee was a teen of the '80s not the '50s when I was a teenager. I was torn between wanting to be a modern Mom but also wanting to protect her. I remember telling her later that evening that she ought to be an adult and very seriously in love with a man before she considered sleeping with him. A discussion about birth control seemed ludicrous at that time when she assured me she thought the whole thing was disgusting. She was back to being my 14-year-old again.

It was challenging for Dee Dee to keep both her social life in BBG and her theater life in Arts going at the same time, but she did. Throughout her high school years, it was like she was living a double life. Rarely did the two spheres cross. The kids in BBG never related to her theatrical life and all the demands it placed on her time. Her BBG friends rarely came to see her perform. Yet she persisted and eventually earned the Star of Deborah, a top achievement award given to those members of BBG with many hours of service to the organization and the community. It is odd but I do not recall her friends from Arts challenging her unavailability on weekends for social activities. Perhaps because they came from all over the city, they, too, reverted back into their social groups in their neighborhoods and churches on those weekends that they weren't in rehearsals or shows.

Dee Dee was disappointed that she was never chosen as a "sweetheart" for any of the B'nai Brith Boys' chapters. She dealt with her disappointment the same way she dealt with rejection from auditions: she would feel bad, real bad, for maybe 24 hours. Then, like a rubber ball, she came bouncing right back. Of all the things that she learned at Arts, accepting rejection was probably the most important skill that she acquired. How many of us can handle rejection with grace and resiliency? It is a fine art.

December 15, 1984

As part of the deal to attend Arts, I promised Mom that I would keep a social life with my Jewish friends. There were times when I found this very frustrating. I have a crush on "Dave" (not his real name), one of the guys I met at a BBG dance. He's real short like me and so cute. We went out a couple of times. All we've done is kiss a little. He'll be leaving for college soon. I was really hurt when he suggested that we just be good friends. I want to be his girlfriend. Maybe I'm not pretty enough or old enough for him.

While I thought Dave was a nice Jewish boy, I wondered why he arrived 45 minutes to an hour late whenever he came to our house to take Dee Dee on a date. I told her that I thought his tardiness was disrespectful and it gave me the feeling that he really did not want to take her out. When I questioned Dee Dee about this she became defensive and offered some lame excuse for his lateness.

In Dee Dee's sophomore year, she began to get meatier roles from the theater department. She played Sarah Brown, little Miss Goody Two Shoes, in *Guys and Dolls*. Every musical theater show was performed in the Experimental Theatre. Dee Dee used to say that even at Arts, musical theater was treated like the stepchild of the theater department. The major productions, the dramas, were held in the main auditorium. Personally, I liked the more intimate setting of the Experimental Theatre and, quite frankly, the seats were much more comfortable than they were in the main auditorium, which was no small point when you attended as many performances as I did. My daughter was at home on a stage. Live theater challenged her and it was quite obvious that she loved it.

Personally, I loved the theater discipline taught at Arts. One Friday after school, I came to a rehearsal to give Dee Dee a ride home. I was early, as usual, so I sat down quietly in the back of the auditorium. The kids on the stage were getting pretty restless and noisy, which is what I would have expected from a group of teenagers on a Friday afternoon. Miss Smith walked in after me and clapped her hands twice and then said, "Boys and girls, if you want a director to fire you on the spot, just keep carrying on." A quiet hushed over the stage. I never saw a group of teenagers snap to attention so fast. This was serious business and they learned a valuable lesson. When the director is speaking, you give her your undivided attention or else.

The students were also taught the discipline of making a "call." If the director sets a call for 5 p.m. and you walk in at 5:05, you are out of the show. For Dee Dee, who was perpetually late, that posed a big challenge, but yet she was never late for a call. No excuse existed for missing or being late for a rehearsal or a performance in the world of theater.

Dee Dee was exposed to the privilege of performance. She performed in many productions at Arts—*The*

Dear Departed, The Madwoman of Chaillot, Dinner, The Wiz, The Dragon and the Gemstones, Nothing to Fear, and *Pippin*, to name a few. She also learned to design and hang lights and to run a light and soundboard. But she considered this "techy work" and her first love was performance. Sometimes Dee Dee used her technical skills to earn a little extra money, like the time she worked for the Dallas Theater Center running their light board. She didn't usually let people know that she had technical skills. She wanted to be an actress. She did not need to be the star. She just wanted to perform. To Dee Dee you were either in front of the lights or behind them and never the twain shall meet!

As she matured, opportunities for Dee Dee's performance talents kept growing. Sure, there were the rejections. For every role she captured, there were many that she did not. Dee Dee's big break came when she was cast as Wendy in a production of *Peter Pan* for the Dallas Children's Theater. Dee Dee, the professional actor, was in love...in love with the stage, musical theater and little kids. She impressed Jonathan, the director for *Peter Pan*, with her dedication and talent.

August 1, 1986

Jonathan got sick after Peter Pan *closed. I wanted to go visit him but two of my teachers from Arts who were very close to him said that he did not want any visitors. I heard that he had pneumonia. When I saw him after he recovered, he looked so thin to me. Rumors were circulating that he had AIDS. Then Jonathan was hospitalized again. I wanted to go visit but again my teachers said that he didn't want any visitors. No one told me he was dying. I wish I had the chance to talk to him before he died. I didn't know much about AIDS and wasn't sure he died from AIDS but it didn't matter to me. I went to his funeral and it was obvious that his family never accepted his gay partner. This made me very angry. He was such a special, gifted soul. For years after he died, I dedicated all my performances, "To Jonathan, who taught me*

how to fly." I hope he somehow knew how much I appreci-
ated and loved him...for teaching me so many ways to fly.

September, my senior year began with Mom pres-
suring me to fill out college applications. With all that I had
learned about theater, I was still a procrastinator, espe-
cially if it came to writing something. Personally, I don't
think I was ready for college. I was having too much fun in
high school. Mom called me her late bloomer. She said I
never seemed ready for the next growth step until I was right
up to the wire. This never bothered me, but it did bug my
Mom.
I didn't have a clue where I wanted to go to college. I
scored pretty low on my SATs. I never tested well and there
were no special provisions on the tests for kids with dyslexia
in those days. The SATs didn't measure creativity or talent,
but they were important criteria for college entrance. I knew
that I didn't want to go to a conservatory, which was a
school that just trained voice, acting, etc. I wanted a well-
rounded liberal arts college education.
Mom was right to stay on my case about those col-
lege apps. I made application to N.Y.U, a school that ap-
pealed to me because it would get me to New York. I also
applied to St. Edward's University in Austin, TX, Webster
University, and the University of Miami because all of them
offered the kind of education I was looking for as well as a
good theater program. Both U. of M. and St. Edward's Uni-
versity sent representatives to Arts to audition students.
I was disappointed when the rejection letter came
from N.Y.U. I knew it was a long shot with my low SAT
scores, but I wanted to go there. Fortunately, Webster Uni-
versity, the University of Miami and St Edward's University
accepted me. I chose the University of Miami mainly because
we had relatives living near the school and I wanted to get
out of Texas. I needed a different scene.
After I accepted the University of Miami, I had sec-
ond thoughts about leaving Dallas. I won't know anyone
there. I'll be far from home. I'll miss Marie...(blah, blah,

grouse, grouse). But you know what? Watch out Miami, because here I come and I'm gonna knock your socks off!

The first time I believed that Dee Dee just might make it in this crazy business called show business was the evening I attended a show that she directed for her senior project at Arts. It was called *Free to Be You and Me*. It was her adaptation of Marlo Thomas' book, *Free to Be Me*. What impressed me the most was her friend, Marie, whom my daughter cast in the lead. It could have been Dee Dee on that stage. If she communicated her style that well to another actor, then she had the gift...the director's eye. The production had her thumbprint all over it. It was amazing to see her dream become reality. Dee Dee had always said, "Someday, I want to direct."

February 1, 1987

One of the most fun things I did in my senior year was my director project. I cast Marie in the lead. We had just met and we hit it off right away. I thought that she was a phenomenal actress and great piano player, someone who oozed energy and talent. By the end of the show's run, we were best friends. Some of my fondest memories of Marie and me, besides singing together, were watching our favorite soap opera, All My Children *(which I jokingly dubbed "All My Kiddies,") and the Tony awards on TV together. We fantasized what it would be like for us to win a Tony.*

We started a tradition of celebrating Christmas in her family's home on Christmas morning. This was so much fun for me since in my house we didn't celebrate Christmas. I became affectionately known as their "Jewish Santa Claus."

During my senior year, except for a great guy-friend, Robby, I pretty much gave up my association and activities with the Jewish youth group. Most of those other kids were really into doing a lot of drinking. I did my fair share of it with them, but didn't really enjoy it. If I didn't go to their parties, I didn't drink.

In my senior year, I started smoking cigarettes because I was cast as Frastrada in Pippin. I continued to smoke on and off after the play closed. I guess I was what you would call a social smoker. Later, I just gave up cigarettes. Compared to the kinds of things some of my other friends were doing, I was a square. My brother knew that I was drinking and smoking and felt that it was his place to lecture me about quitting every chance he got. I thought I did a pretty good job of hiding it from Mom but I'll bet now that she really knew.

April 1987

Senior year also meant Senior Trip. I loved traveling to London in the spring with my class and my AP English teacher, Dr. Donna. She and her husband were chaperones and they were great fun. I especially enjoyed Covent Gardens and the London theater scene. We saw Cats *and* Starlight Express. *I found a new love—traveling. After that, Mom said I always had my suitcase packed and was ready to go when any opportunity to travel was available and she was right!*

June 1987

My graduation from Arts was unique and inspiring. I received awards in directing, lighting design and musical theater along with my diploma. We performed for our graduation exercises. Parts of me were happy to be graduating and parts of me were sad about leaving Arts and my best friend, Marie. My decision to go to Arts had been so right for me. I didn't think that any school could ever duplicate the wonderful experiences I had there.

Dee Dee was a woman-child of many paradoxes. She wanted to go to college outside of Texas and then she acted like a kid who was sorry that she decided to go so far away from home. We fought over one thing or another her whole senior year. I hoped that her moodiness and contrary behavior were just a part of her inner struggle to become emotionally independent from the family.

It reminded me of the time when Dee Dee was 10. She was the first person in our family to encourage me to go back into the professional work world. It had been years since I taught school and I had no desire to return to it. I re-entered with a part-time personnel job. After I started working, Dee Dee was the person in the family who complained the most. She missed me and was the least cooperative about doing her fair share of the workload at home. She always seemed to need that little extra attention, encouragement or hug. She was my huggy bear.

July 1987

After I graduated from Arts, I spent the summer in performance. I did The Dragon and the Gemstones, *which was performed in Dallas and Los Angeles. My first taste of L.A. Ugh, give me New York. In fact, I was so busy that summer I hardly had time to pack up all my stuff for college. Mom and Dad could never relate to my last-minute packing. My folks were always so organized. Even my brother was Mr. Organized. Me, I was Miss Spontaneous and Queen of the Last Minute!*

Another reason that I dragged my feet was that I did not want to say goodbye to Marie. Marie had another two years at Arts so I knew that when I returned to Dallas, we could get together. She reminded me that we would celebrate Christmas in her home. Yes, we would always have Christmas. But Christmas seemed so far away. Why did I choose to go to college two thousand miles away? Some days it was difficult to remember my reason for that decision.

Chapter Thirteen

A REAL DIFFERENT SCENE
August 1987-1989

The scene when we arrived at the University of Miami was chaotic. We went to my cousin's home first to pick up Dee Dee's boxes. We were lucky to have family living in Miami who received and stored all of them for us until we arrived, and they even helped us transport her stuff to her dorm. Guess they were only too happy to have their living room floor back.

Her dorm room was an austere cinder block room with two narrow beds, two closets, and two dressers for two students. The communal bathroom was down the hall. We helped Dee Dee make her room homier by setting up her TV, laying down some carpeting and tacking up some posters on the walls on her half of the room. After that, we accompanied her to the Campus Theater for a new student orientation.

September 1, 1987
The first teacher I met at U. of M. called me "Miss Fields." Mom said I would be more comfortable if she called me "Dee Dee." The teacher snapped back at Mom in an icy tone, "Here she will be known as Miss Fields." Mom knew right away that I was in the wrong place, but she didn't say anything to me at that time. She sensed that I was apprehensive and it wouldn't have taken much to put me over the edge. It took me a lot longer time to figure out that I was in

*the wrong school. During orientation I was told that fresh-
men were not allowed to perform. At first I didn't think it
would be any big deal.*

April 1, 1988

    *I'm dying to perform on a stage, again! My teachers
here have been tearing me down all year. They say that they
need to strip me of all my bad habits. Humph. I auditioned
for a production of* Peace Child *when I was in Dallas last
month. God, I hope I get it.*

    *The tour is this summer for six weeks. At 19 I'm a lit-
tle old for the show but I still look 16. I know that most of the
cast will be younger than I am, but I don't care. I need to
perform and if I get cast in* Peace Child *I'll get to travel the
Soviet Union. I desperately need to be inspired.*

    Marie did a tour of Peace Child *last summer and
she's still raving about it. Mom's concerned because the tour
ends a day before my classes begin in Miami. No problem, I
told her. I'll just fly directly from New York to school and not
return to Dallas. Mom's such a worrywart.*

    When Dee Dee completed her freshman year at the
University of Miami, I thought she might transfer to another
college because she sounded unhappy with the program. She
said it was more of a conservatory-type program and she
wanted a liberal arts approach to her college education. She
surprised me when she announced that she planned to return
to Miami for her sophomore year.

    Then she told me about her plan to do a *Peace Child*
tour during the summer. I knew this was not very practical
because the end of the tour and the beginning of the fall semester in college were one day apart. The age-old tug of war
played within me. Do I let her do the tour and suffer the potential consequences when she returns, or do I just say "no"?
She wanted to do it. "Roots and wings," I told myself, "let
her go."

    Dee Dee always wanted to use her talent for a greater
purpose. The purpose of *Peace Child* was to use theater and

children to deliver a powerful message to the political leaders both in the United States and the Soviet Union to eliminate their weapons of mass destruction and make peace for the children's futures. If Dee Dee did not do the tour this year, she would be too old to do it next year. Roots and wings.

After Dee Dee left the country for the tour, I remember feeling so alone and cut off from her. Even though the University of Miami was 2,000 miles from Dallas, she and I remained close throughout her freshman year thanks to frequent telephone conversations and visits. When she was home for the summer break, a summer now shortened by six weeks, we stuffed in a mother/daughter spa vacation in Austin and enjoyed doing some theater, shopping and lunching in Dallas before her tour. When she was gone, I knew that I could have called the chaperones of the tour, but I was reluctant to do that unless there was an emergency situation. A lonely mom was not exactly an emergency. It was the first time that we could not talk to each other for six solid weeks, which felt interminable.

When the tour ended, Dee Dee placed a call to me right after she landed in New York before she caught her connecting flight to Miami. I was relieved to hear her voice and to know that she was back on American soil. She had an unbelievable tour experience and was riding high.

"I'll call you when I get to school, Mom." She sounded so grown-up to me. Maybe, there was hope yet that this child, my baby, would mature into an adult." My daughter gave me many moments of doubt as to whether she would ever mature. Surely she was on a much longer time line than my son, but on this day she sounded as if she would actually make it.

September 3, 1988

What can I say about Peace Child*? It was awesome. For the first time I performed in order to send a message, a message of peace. It was both the hardest and the best six weeks of my life at the same time. The kids I met were tal-*

121

ented and charming. Because I was older than most of them and had more performance experience, I was asked to be the assistant director. What fun!

Touring St. Basil's Cathedral in Moscow was one of the many highlights of the tour but so was the Black Sea and performing for the Politburo. During the tour stop at the Black Sea, I met a young Russian man, Serge, on whom I developed a crush. I think he was KGB because he never let any of us take his picture and he didn't really have anything to do with the tour. I told Mom I think of him as the spy who loved me. He helped me with my Russian and listened to me talk about missing my family and friends back home. It was hard being separated from them and not being able to share my experiences with them until I returned to America. When the tour was nearing the end, I gave my new Soviet friends my jeans and sneakers because they couldn't purchase those things very easily. When the tour ended, we cried and cried knowing that after we parted, we would never see each other again. The Soviet kids gave me little buttons and treasures that I cherish as souvenirs. When I arrived in the States, the first thing I did was call Mom. I was sorry that I had to go straight back to Miami but didn't tell Mom that.

After Dee Dee returned to Miami, she sounded despondent. She said the kids at school were the problem. Much later I learned it was much more than that. At the time I thought Dee Dee just needed to talk about *Peace Child* and that the problem was her friends were not interested in hearing about it. Every time she called home, she was crying.

"Maybe she's just having a problem adjusting to university life after her special summer experience," I remarked to Howard. "I don't like how she sounds. I'm going to ask my cousins to keep an eye on her."

"Don't worry. I'm sure she's okay," Howard replied trying to calm my worries.

By November I was very concerned and suggested that she consider leaving the University of Miami and return to Dallas. She said that she would not quit school in the middle of the semester. After giving it some thought, a few days later she called again.

"Mom, I've made a decision. I'm going to finish out this semester. Then I'm going to come back to Dallas and take a semester at a junior college. Next fall, I think I want to go to St. Edward's University in Austin."

Her plan sounded reasonable to me. I complimented her for thinking it all out—another sign that she was growing up, however painful that process was.

When she returned home, she told Howard and me that she was no longer interested in studying theater. "All I want to do is to take some liberal arts courses. Maybe I'll major in political science." At the time I was angry with her teachers in Miami. I thought that they had broken her spirit for the theater.

Shortly after returning home, she decided to visit her high school just to say hello to some of her former teachers. To her surprise one of her teachers offered her a job teaching a lighting class. She accepted it. Then, after work one day, she stopped by the Dallas Children's Theater just to say hello to the people she knew there. They were thrilled that she was back in Dallas. The owner of the theater and one of her directors encouraged Dee Dee to audition. She did leading roles in *Prodigy*; *Tales of a Fourth Grade Nothing*; and *The Lion, The Witch and The Wardrobe* that spring semester. The old bubbly, upbeat Dee Dee returned. She enjoyed her classes and performing for the Dallas Children's Theater. Near the end of the semester, she explored the idea of going to St. Edward's University in Austin for her junior year.

January 5, 1989

I can't tell Mom what really happened to me at U. of M. I can't even talk about it with Marie. Everyone has a partial picture of the truth. It is true that the kids in Miami were very unenthusiastic about my summer with Peace Child*. I guess I did need time to debrief after my tour, but it just couldn't be that way. I was miserable enough and then there was that horrible date.*

I didn't want to go the party but my friends convinced me that it would be good for me. This guy I knew asked me if I was going. When I said yes, he winked at me and said that he would see me there. I was actually in a pretty good mood the night of the party until the incident happened. The guy and I danced. There was lots of booze at the party but I did not have all that much to drink. It was no big deal for me to drink, because I had done my fair share of it in high school.

I'm not sure how this guy got me on the couch alone but there we were. He started to kiss me and I told him to stop. But he didn't stop. In the next few minutes he unzipped his pants and forced my head down on his lap and held me there until he came. I spit and ran out of the party hysterical. There was so much noise from the music and laughter that no one even noticed when I left. I was so grateful that the guy didn't come after me.

I ran back to my dorm room (thankfully, my roommate wasn't there), threw myself across my bed and bawled like a baby. I was terribly distraught and wondered what I had done that made the guy force himself on me. I didn't tell anyone about the incident because I felt somehow responsible for the whole thing. I was inconsolable and stayed that way for weeks until I finally decided to return to Dallas. I didn't want to quit school, but I could barely function in Miami after that incident. Through some miracle, I passed all of my courses last semester.

February 8, 1989

It feels great to be back home with a chance to regroup. My classes in junior college are easy compared to the ones I took at Miami and it's a relief not to be taking any theater classes. My Peace Child experience is making me think that maybe I'd like a career in politics. Those University of Miami teachers really attacked my self-esteem. Maybe the theater isn't for me.

I was hired by Arts to teach and it really has lifted my spirits. I like being a teacher and making some money. After work the other day, I stopped by the Dallas Children's Theater. *Robyn encouraged me to audition and thanks to John, I think I'll get cast into some shows.*

May 1, 1989

Living at home and acting for Dallas Children's Theater *is what I did before I left for college. This scene is all too familiar and comfortable just like an old shoe. I need to move on, to grow, which is why I've reapplied to St. Ed's. I'm going to visit the school next weekend and talk to the people in the administration. I am glad that Mom made me follow through with a letter to them after they accepted me, even though I had decided to go to the U. of M. when I was a freshman.*

May 15, 1989

The people at St. Ed's were so friendly and helpful. They encouraged me to continue as a theater major. The school has an equity theater, where I could earn points toward my actors' union equity card from their productions. And perhaps most enticing of all was they would accept all of my credits from Miami and junior college. If I'm a theater major I can start my junior year of college next semester, and finish school in two years with a Bachelor of Arts degree in theater. It all made perfect sense to me, so when I returned to Dallas, I told my folks what I planned to do. "Mom, I've decided to go to St. Ed's next semester. And, by the way, I'm going to major in theater." She just smiled.

I've given a lot of thought to that really bad date during these last few months at home. I wish I could talk to Mom about it but I feel so ashamed and frightened. I feel frozen with fear and embarrassment. How could I have been so stupid? I blame myself, even though I told the guy "no." Why did he just keep going? Why didn't I kick him or yell for help? This just confirms my thinking—guys are stupid jerks. I don't need a guy. But, then I watch the soaps on TV and wonder how all those people enjoy making love. It is perplexing. Marie told me that she had been date-raped when she was in high school, but it hasn't stopped her from being sexually active and she's three years younger than I am. She said that some day I'll find a guy that I'll like and I'll want to do it. Me? Yuck! Never.

***

St. Edward's University became a positive, memorable college experience for me. So when Al and I talked about going public, I told him that I wanted to go back to Texas to speak at my synagogue, high school and college in Austin. Besides wanting to do our AIDS 101 presentation for the kids, I knew deep down in my heart that I would be visiting my teachers and schools probably for the last time.

So after our sessions at my synagogue and high school in Dallas, we drove down to Austin to visit St. Ed's. How many times had I driven down that road?

Chapter Fourteen

THE ACTOR'S LIFE FOR ME
September 1989-June 1991

The city of Austin is approximately 200 miles from Dallas. Dee Dee could make the car trip from St. Edward's University in three-and-a-half hours whenever she felt the need to touch base back home. I counted the number of trips she made to Dallas during her junior year of college. She came home about nine times or about once a month, but I was happy that she was living at school again and her life appeared to be back on track.

September 3, 1989

I told Dad that he didn't have to drive me to St. Ed's. I was, after all, an upperclassman and didn't need my Daddy to take me to school. But after I assembled all my stuff for the move, I asked him at the last minute, "Dad, could you caravan drive with me back to school?" I know that Mom was exasperated because I always changed my mind at the last minute. I hate to admit it, but Mom was right. I'd bite off more than I could chew and then I'd have to backpedal. I'd get pretty bitchy with Mom as if it was her fault. My brother lectured me often about the way I talked back to Mom; this did not make me any happier. I fought with Mom because I wanted to make my own decisions. Then when things went wrong, like the time I returned to U. of M. directly after my

Peace Child *tour, I'd get all frustrated and take it out on her. I screwed up again but Mom wouldn't say "I told you so." She didn't have to say it because I felt it. I'm just a right-brained kid who was dropped into a left-brained family. I fought with Daddy, too, but with him it was different. The person I listened to the best was my closest friend, Marie. When I left for St. Ed's, Marie left Dallas for Duke University. There would be miles between us, but we stayed close over the years of separation thanks to the U.S. mail and the telephone.*

I have to admit when Dee Dee moved to Austin, I was relieved. I loved her, but living with Dee Dee the actress was challenging. She was mercurial, up one minute and down the next. Her life was always full of drama and tumult. When Dee Dee hit our house, it was a like a white tornado had blown through it. Her things were everywhere. She would sleep late in the morning and keep erratic evening hours.

On the other hand, she would light up our home with her zest for life, her warm heart and music. She and her friends, always an interesting array of characters, would sometimes perform, but most often practice, in our living room. Her friends were like her—very warm and loving.

I visited Dee Dee at St. Ed's after she had been in school for about a month. She introduced me to a nice group of actor friends. Her small university, another cocoon, reminded me of the Arts Magnet High School. She quickly developed a bond with the head of the theater department that became a mutual admiration. Dee Dee's talents were being appreciated and opportunities for her to perform developed rapidly. After one semester in a dormitory, she decided to move into her first apartment off campus. I felt proud of my daughter. Dee Dee was growing into a capable young woman even if it was by fits and starts.

Dee Dee's talent was also maturing. When she sang a song, it was as if she reached down into her toes and stuffed all 95 pounds of her body into her voice. It was thrilling. Her

128

talent, acting out the lyrics of a song, was also growing. She did leading roles in the *Mystery of Edwin Drood, Life with Father* and *Chicago*. She was cast against type in St. Ed's productions. Her talents were stretched by positive reinforcement, not by breaking down her self-esteem. As Roxy Hart in *Chicago*, she played a murderous vamp! This was not the same Dee Dee who was just doing children's theater, or was it?

November 15, 1989

My junior year at St. Ed's so far is great. I've made friends easily and I'm enjoying the theater department. My classes are interesting and challenging. I've had a date or two with Danny. I'm taking it slow because I'm scared to death. I know I have to grow up and get over this thing I have about sex. Maybe I'll call my high school boyfriend, Dave, in New York and next summer we can get together. I'm nursing this fantasy that I visit him and we make love. Next time I'm home I'll see my gynecologist and get on the pill so I'll be safe.

I just met a nice guy named Patrick a few weeks ago in the St. Ed's bookstore where he works. He's a student here too. I'm the stage manager for Love by the Bolt. *Maybe I can get him a role in the production. I'm attracted to his bedroom brown eyes, handsome Italian face and warm personality. He had enrolled at St. Ed's thinking that he wanted the Seminary. His teachers felt that he was not suited to the priesthood and suggested that he find another major. I suggested acting. From the moment we met we've become great friends. We have so much in common except, of course, for our religious backgrounds. He's a good Catholic boy from New Orleans. Who else am I going to meet at St. Ed's? We went to the Unity Church of Austin last Sunday. I love the metaphysical pathway to God. I'm going to church with him next weekend.*

May 15, 1990

My junior year is almost over. I've auditioned for summer stock for a theater in Granbury, Texas. I'll be lucky to get the work. Patrick and I have grown close. I'm not happy about leaving him in Austin for the summer.

June 14, 1990

I'm planning to go to New York for a short vacation. Dave invited me to stay with him. After I return I'll move to Granbury for the summer to do The Ziegfeld Follies *and* 42nd Street *in summer stock.*

July 1, 1990

I lived out my fantasy! Dave and I did it. He was kind and gentle. We parted as old friends. I knew Dave wasn't interested in a relationship. (Later that year, I bumped into Dave in, of all places, a gay bar in Austin, and then all the pieces finally fit together.)

I'm so miserable here in Granbury. I think my director is an alcoholic and she only cast me in a chorus part. I spend most of my time thinking about Patrick. I miss him and wonder if he misses me in the same way. I can't wait until I return to St. Ed's in the fall. I'm hoping we'll become even closer and more intimate.

September 30, 1990

I started my senior year anticipating this great relationship. I'm disappointed because Patrick, while affectionate, doesn't respond to me sexually. There must be something wrong with me. I've heard rumors about Patrick, but I don't believe them.

December 10, 1990

I'm in shock! Patrick told me last night that he was gay. We're performing in a production of La Cage aux Folles. *He was really acting "out" the other night at rehearsal. I've never seen him act that way and it crushed me. I know that I scared Mom was when I called her a little while ago to tell her about Patrick and I was crying again.*

January 5, 1991

I'm sure when my folks came to Austin to see me in the show last week they knew how much I needed them. It took all the courage I had to get on stage with Patrick. After the show, the stage was converted into a real cabaret. I sat on a stool and sang to the audience and thanked my parents for their love and support. I dedicated Wind Beneath My Wings *to them. I know they got my message because when the lights came up, I saw tears rolling down their cheeks.*

I wasn't quite sure if my daughter's relationship with Patrick was just a manifestation of her imagination or he led her to believe that it was more, but it didn't matter. She was terribly disappointed when she learned that he was gay. "Oh, no," I thought, "Dee Dee's heading back into that black hole she found at University of Miami." I wanted to kill Patrick for hurting her.

Howard and I drove to Austin mainly to be with her. We did not want her to be alone on New Year's Eve. As a bonus we saw her show. After the show, she sang *Wind Beneath My Wings* to us. It was the first time she had ever publicly sung a song to us. We were so moved that we cried.

After the show closed Dee Dee returned home to lick her wounds. Fortunately it was semester break. By the time she returned to school in mid-January, she and Patrick had talked it through and made amends. They graduated as the best of friends. It took me a lot longer to forgive him for what appeared to me to be an act of leading her on and hurting her.

April 20, 1991

I can't believe that I'll be graduating next month! I have to make some decision about what I want to do next. I could stay in Austin and do some performing. But I would be a big fish in a little pond. Or I could try New York and be a small fish in a big pond. I keep hearing the words of my voice coach in Dallas. She would say, "I wish I had gone to New York when I was young. Now I'm too old and I have too many responsibilities. I'll never know if I could've made it in the Big Apple."

Mom was pretty negative about New York when I visited N.Y.U but I was 18 at that time. I'm 22 and have lived away from home and traveled abroad. Surely Mom would be more receptive to a move to New York now.

Some of my friends at St. Edward's are auditioning for New York acting academies. Recruiters from those schools are coming to Austin to look for students. I'm not thrilled with the concept of more schooling, but if it gets me to New York, it might be worth it. I know that I floored my folks when I told them that I was going to audition for the American Music and Dramatic Academy. "Mom, if I'm accepted then I could fine-tune my dance skills. I could become a triple threat (someone who sings, acts and dances)."

Mom understood. My voice and acting were my leading strengths. While I could move on stage, I was not much of a dancer. This is partly because of my body type—short legs and big boobs is not your ideal dancer's body. And, my not-so-great coordination was another reality of my learning challenges. My goal would be to develop professional dance skills. If I'm going to be successful on Broadway I know that I have to do it all. I know some of the schools in New York had connections just like the Arts Magnet High School did in Dallas. It wouldn't guarantee anything, but attending AMDA might begin to work me into the New York scene.

May 1, 1991

Well, I gave it a shot. I'll know in a couple of days if I made it.

May 5, 1991

I am elated. My name appeared on the short acceptance list posted by AMDA. The recruiter made me very aware that the school only accepts a handful of students from across the country. I'm so proud of myself and excited about the chance to study in New York.

When Dee Dee told me about AMDA, I was pleasantly surprised. After all, this was my kid who hated going to school. This was my child who was learning-challenged. I prayed for her to just make it through college.

When she called to tell me that she was accepted, I was so happy for her. I still had plenty of trepidation about her move to New York in July of '91. But I was the one who always told her to follow her dreams. There was no holding back my gutsy little girl. I had to admire her spunk even if she did give me most of my gray hairs. Dee Dee, my born actress, talked, prepared and dreamed about Broadway all of her life. I knew that if she did not make this move to New York, she would always regret it. So what is a mother to do? I helped her pack.

Chapter Fifteen

MAKING GOOD MEMORIES
Fall 1994-Spring 1995

November 20, 1994
Al and I were pleased with our presentation at St. Ed's. As we drove back to Dallas, I reflected on how wonderful '94 had been in spite of all of my health challenges. We had a beautiful wedding, honeymooned on Maui and bought an adorable house. And, I had just had the wonderful opportunities to speak at my synagogue, high school and college.

My health is pretty good on D4T. I feel better than I ever felt on AZT. I think I even look a little better. I'm still pretty thin but not gaunt. I'm looking forward to my reunion with Marie when Al and I return to Dallas at Christmas. Al and I are going to perform the show we've developed for Hearts and Voices for my parents and their friends. We'll ring in 1995 with my folks. As 1994 draws to a close, I'm feeling pretty darn good about my life, all things considered.

Dee Dee and Al's visit over the Christmas holidays was a fun way to end the year. They performed their 45-minute cabaret show for a small gathering of 50 of our closest friends. The show was delightfully entertaining but it hurt me to observe the "not-so-obvious-to-others" signs of my daughter's compromised performance skills. The HIV had already weakened the muscles she used to support her voice. Her stamina was substantially reduced, too. I had never seen Dee Dee sit down during any performances until that night. To the friends gathered in our home that evening, the show was most enjoyable.

Dee Dee introduced the show that she and Al put together for a Denver version of Hearts and Voices, a group that originated in New York of performers who entertained AIDS and other terminally ill patients in hospitals and hospices. Dee Dee smiled when she said, "I told Al, I need to do this show for a different crowd."

So lucky us, we were the recipients of their comedic acting and combined musical talents. One of our friends remarked the show was as good as anything he had seen recently on Broadway. It became the last of our great living room concerts.

Dee Dee and Al brought to Dallas copies of a second recording of songs that they had made. They titled the audiocassette, *Rainbow Wishes*. It was different from their first tape, *Choices*, with its Broadway and popular tunes. *Rainbow Wishes* had been recorded to entertain Dee Dee's nephew, Ben, so it was primarily a collection of Disney songs. Dee Dee told me she liked studio recording because it was easy for her to do with her diminished performance capacity. Between takes, if she needed, she could rest on the couch in the studio. She did not have to put full power to her voice either. In fact, she needed to learn to throttle back her voice when she was on a microphone in a recording studio or she would overpower the equipment.

After that visit, I wrote the family another one of my famous family letters. I said, "It is so gratifying to see her and to hear Dee Dee's spirit reflected on the tape *Rainbow Wishes.* She is happy, upbeat and probably in the best place emotionally since her diagnosis. She lives her life with zest. Her health is fairly stable even though she continues to experience great fatigue and an annoying array of HIV symptoms like indigestion, oral sores, and yeast infections. So far, the major complications of AIDS have been held at bay. We aren't kidding ourselves; we are painfully aware of the sword that still hangs precariously over our heads. We are so thankful for these good hours, days and weeks and pray for them to continue. Hold us in your prayers. Your love sustains us all."

Reflecting on that letter, I realize now how prophetic it was. None of us knew what the new year would bring, which was good because nothing in all that we had experienced could have prepared us for the year to come.

The year started on a high note when in January of '95 we met Dee Dee and Al in Miami for a vacation. A few days later they drove down to the Florida Keys for a day to swim with the dolphins. Dee Dee dreamed of doing this and it gave me great pleasure to make arrangements for the swim. When I had made the reservations months prior, I told the proprietor that Dee Dee had AIDS because there was a non-refundable deposit, and we could not guarantee that she would be well enough to travel on any one specific date. The man understood and waived the deposit. He said that he had a special healing program for people like her and he offered it to us at no charge. I was touched by his generosity.

We were on a quest to make good memories. Repeatedly, Dee Dee said that she would not live her life in a bubble even if her immune system were virtually nonexistent. She wanted to travel, to be with people and to swim with the dolphins. Of course as her mom, I feared that she was taking unnecessary risks, but at the same time, parts of me understood her desire to appear healthy and normal. She adamantly proclaimed, "I refuse to be an AIDS victim. I am a person living with AIDS." And she boldly lived her life to underline that statement. On another level, I was proud of her courage in adversity. She taught me more about life and living then anyone or anything I had experienced thus far.

January 30, 1995

I loved swimming with the dolphins in the Florida Keys. I'm not the strong swimmer I once was, which was a bit disconcerting, but I had a great time. My instructor said not to use my arms when I swam with the dolphins. It was a physical challenge to only use my legs to swim. Apparently dolphins don't like waving arms. Al and I were fitted into wet suits and I plunged right into the cold water. Al hesitated a moment. The dolphins must have sensed my need. They swam by my side and nuzzled with me. I feel renewed in a way that defies description.

February 18, 1995

I'm so angry with Mom and Dad. Why? Well, they're always researching HIV. So when they went to California for a convention last week, they decided to take a little side trip and didn't tell me about it. They visited with Dr. Alexandra Levine, a renowned researcher in the field of women and HIV. They felt lucky to get an appointment with her. After they spoke to her, they told me about the visit. I felt so betrayed. Why? Because this is MY disease and any decision about it is going to be my decision not theirs!

Dr. Levine suggested that I take one of the new viral load tests. This test would measure the amount of HIV in my blood. At that time, the doctors were not sure how the numbers the test provided would translate clinically, but the test could be used to judge whether the medication I'm taking is effective. If the viral load increases it means the drug I'm on isn't working. The test could be used as an indicator to change my medication. My folks also learned about the new class of HIV drugs, protease inhibitors that were soon-to-be-made available for the sickest AIDS patients. Mom and Dad sounded so excited with the promising news. I know that I exasperated them when I just rejected all this stuff. I must have sounded like I didn't want to save myself. Maybe I'm afraid to believe that some miracle treatment is close at hand.

April 10, 1995

I asked Dr. Judy about running a viral load test on me today. She didn't encourage me to do it for two reasons. One, she suspected that the number would be very high and it would send me into another emotional tailspin like the time when I learned I had zero T-cells, but two, more importantly, the newer treatments weren't available yet. We discussed the protease inhibitors. The first one, Saquinavir, was going to be available in a few months. She said that she would talk to me about changing my regimen at that time. She saw no reason to take me off D4T since I was doing pretty well on it or so it appeared.

I expected Dee Dee to be upset with Howard and me for seeing Dr. Levine because we did not discuss it with her before we did it. I was not sure that we would actually get to talk with the doctor and I did not want to discuss it with her because I suspected that she would not want us to do it. She was angry with us, but the good thing about Dee Dee was she would get angry and then blow it off. From the beginning of our perilous journey with HIV, it was obvious that we had different styles of coping. The more I read and learned about HIV, the more empowered I felt. It kept hope alive and it helped me to get through the night. As the famous football coach from Notre Dame, Ara Parseghian, once said, "Keep hope in your heart and never give up."

Dee Dee wanted to control this last remnant of her existence. I felt more in control when I understood more. My daughter sometimes felt overwhelmed by knowledge. She would often say, "I'm taking a holiday from HIV." That meant she did not want to think about it or talk about it, at least for that day.

Early in her journey, Dee Dee faced the inevitable. She only took the FDA-approved medications, especially the ones given to protect her from the opportunistic infections. Howard and I wanted her to consider clinical trials and cutting edge treatments but she would not hear of it. It created great tension between us. I kept telling myself that she was an adult. Right or wrong, she made her own choices about her treatments and her life. She may have been 26 years old and a married woman but to me, my daughter was my child. As her mom, all I wanted was for her to live, and I felt frustrated because I did not know how to make that happen. If I was in her place, I do not know how brave I would have been about putting something into my body that no one could tell me for certain what it would do. Her life was slipping through our fingers and there was nothing we could do about it.

While Dee Dee never thought of herself as a victim of HIV, I did, until I attended the First National Mothers March against AIDS held over Mother's Day weekend in '95. Howard and I met Dee Dee and Al in Washington, D.C. to do the march. The purpose of the march was to raise awareness and to address our congressional people for the continuation of Ryan White funding for AIDS research. I was not then, nor do I consider myself today, a political activist. I was just a mom with a daughter with AIDS.

We met Dee Dee and Al at the hotel in D.C. the day before the march. It was going to be a special weekend. My daughter and her husband were invited to sing and speak at the rally. A candlelight service was held at the All Souls Unitarian Church on Friday evening. After we ate a leisurely dinner together, we proceeded to the church. I felt like a stranger in a foreign land until I met Beverly, the group organizer. She gave me the warmest hug. Her daughter, Iris, had died from AIDS just four years before. We bonded immediately. The crowd at the church kept swelling. My daughter sat there. She seemed uncomfortable. "Are you okay, honey?" I asked.

"Sometimes when I'm in a group like this and everyone is dealing with the virus, it just feels more real. When I'm in other groups where people are not living with HIV, I can get away from it for awhile, you know, like a vacation from HIV." She smiled.

"It is just the opposite for me. Most people don't understand what life is like for me, except for maybe the people in the parents support group or the Jewish HIV support group. The people here tonight, they know how I feel. It's comforting not to be alone." We hugged and I thanked her for coming to the Walk.

The ceremony began. Everyone was asked to walk past the microphone and to tell the group their name and where they lived. Most people stepped up to the mike and mumbled. Some people only stated their first name. Even here, people were afraid for others to know who they were. "How sad," I thought. There were approximately 500 people in the room and we were the only ones from Texas. Dee Dee and Al were the only ones from Colorado. People came from all across the country—Ohio, Alabama, Illinois, Washington, New York, New Jersey, California, Florida, Nebraska and even as far as Hawaii. It was a happening and I found myself swept up into it.

I will never forget when Dee Dee stepped up to the microphone. She clearly stated, "We are Dee Dee and Al McKittrick from Denver and we want to thank my parents for bringing us here." Ever the professional, even under those circumstances, Dee Dee pulled on my heartstrings.

A small reception followed the ceremony. Dee Dee felt too tired to attend so she and Al returned to the hotel. I remember thinking, "Damn that disease. Dee Dee who loved socializing with people didn't have the energy to do it!"

Howard and I enjoyed meeting the people gathered at the reception. There were parents of gay sons and moms who had lost heterosexual daughters because of drug abuse. Interestingly, I did not meet another mom of a heterosexual married daughter who contracted HIV from heterosexual transmission. Perhaps that is because it was 1995.

Following the reception, Howard and I returned to our hotel. Too wound up to sleep, we talked late into the night and fell asleep in each other's arms, holding each other so tightly. It was both wonderful and sad to be with moms and dads whose lives, much like ours, had been irreversibly changed by AIDS.

The next day we gathered at the Washington Monument. People carried placards...pictures of their lost sons and daughters. Young mothers with pictures of their lost babies—all the beautiful young children, handsome young men and attractive young women—all gone from AIDS. It was so sad. Would I return here next year with my daughter's picture on a stick? I hoped not.

The singing began, as did my feelings of empowerment. Somehow Howard and I were chosen to lead the parade. Dee Dee was too weak to do the march. She and Al planned to meet us at the rally in Lafayette Park across from the White House.

As we marched I wondered, "How did we get here?" Looking around I saw hundreds of people marching, tourists joining us, as well as a police escort. The short geographic walk to the White House was the longest walk I had taken emotionally thus far. For the first time I was public. The sun was shining and I remember thinking, "God is smiling on us today." I knew in my heart that the lost sons and daughters were smiling with pride on us, too, as they watched their moms, dads, brothers, sisters, nieces, nephews, and friends marching to honor their memory.

At the White House we stopped and lined up shoulder to shoulder. "A moment of silence," one of the organizers requested. I thought, "Is anyone home? Do you care? Do you see all these normal people who have lost their children?" The silence was deafening. We were all alone with our thoughts, as we stood there melded together spiritually. We then proceeded into Lafayette Park where we were reunited with Dee Dee and Al. It was almost time for the rally to start.

"Oh, Mom," Dee Dee cried. "I don't ever want to be a picture on a stick!" I hugged her tightly and promised her I would never do that.

The program began with a 15-year-old boy's speech. He looked about 10 and reminded me of Ryan White. All his life he had been battling AIDS. He received thunderous applause after his presentation. Then a young woman stepped to the podium and read poems written by Iris, Beverly's daughter. The speaker had lived with AIDS for four years. She looked pretty healthy to me though certainly I knew looks could be deceiving with this disease.

Just before it was our turn to speak, a young woman stopped Dee Dee. The woman was crying. She asked my daughter to dedicate her song, "Somewhere Over the Rainbow" to her 4-year-old daughter, Brittany, who had died from AIDS a few months before. The mom told Dee Dee that when Brittany was 2 years old, she saw the movie the *Wizard of Oz*. When the film changed from black-and-white to color, she told her mother that must be heaven. When the mom took Brittany home from the hospital to die, she told Brittany that she would soon be going to heaven. Just before she died the little girl said, "Mommy, I'm going to heaven. I'm going over the rainbow." My daughter's voice was laden with tears, as she dedicated her song to Brittany, after she had shared the story with the crowd. I am still not sure how she gathered her composure to sing that day, but she did.

After the rally we walked to a nearby restaurant for some lunch. Dee Dee could barely make it there. AIDS might have stolen her energy, but never her passion. When we returned to our hotel, we were all totally wiped out. We slept for the remainder of the afternoon. When we awoke, the four of us were so drained that we ordered dinner into our rooms.

The following morning we felt revived as we prepared for the breakfast reception at the Rayburn House. "Today," I told Howard with a big smile on my face "Mr. and Mrs. Fields go to Capitol Hill. I cannot believe that I am here and that we are doing this."

Our first appointment was with Senator Kay Bailey Hutchinson's young legislative assistant. She was a well-dressed woman, all business-like. She greeted us rather coolly. After she heard our story, this 28-year-old woman had tears in her eyes. I am sure she was thinking we could have just as easily been her parents. She assured us that the Senator supported AIDS research programs, as well as the

Ryan White Care Act. At least I felt that I had put a human face, my face, on this disease.

We returned to the closing breakfast reception where we met Dee Dee and Al. They had just spoken to Representative Pat Schroeder's legislative assistant. We remarked about the conservative atmosphere we detected. I wondered what it would take for our political leaders to see AIDS as a disease and not as a moral or social issue. Do their children need to become infected and die before anything will ever get done? Needless to say, our politicians were masters at making us feel supported, but were we?

As the reception drew to a close, we hugged and exchanged phone numbers and addresses with our newfound compatriots as we said our goodbyes. We all knew in our hearts that so much remained to be done, but we had cast our small grains of sand upon a huge beach and I was proud to be part of the happening.

After the reception, the four of us played tourist with the balance of our day. When we separated at the airport, we hugged and kissed. We had made another good memory. Why did it have to be this way? In my heart, I promised Dee Dee and Al and all the other Dee Dees and Als out there that there will be a cure—if not tomorrow, then the day after that or the day after that. For as long as I live I will work toward that day.

On the flight back to Dallas, I was both exhausted and exhilarated. For the first time since Dee Dee had been diagnosed, I no longer felt like a victim of AIDS because I had done something about it. In all this darkness, a small flame of hope flickered in my heart.

Dee Dee and Al celebrated their first wedding anniversary in March of '95. Our gift to them was a cruise to Alaska in July for the family. Howard had wanted to take this trip for many years and Dee Dee expressed the same interest. We invited Alan and his family but they declined because they felt Ben at 20 months old was too young to take on a cruise.

We made our plans early in the year and chose July for the trip because it was the optimum time of the year to take a cruise of the Inside Passage. Dee Dee took such delight in it. We arranged a stateroom for her and Al near the elevators on the ship to minimize her walking, and we planned to do the easier port tours. Before Dee Dee and Al left Denver they had to put some finishing touches on a very special project.

June 12, 1995

The summer of '95 began innocently. We returned to Denver from the Mothers March all invigorated. Of course I had to sleep for several days after the trip to recuperate. I never told Mom about those down days. I knew that she worried so much about me.

Al and I are looking forward to taking our first cruise in July with the folks. We got a call from Arapahoe House, a home for teenage kids at risk. They asked us to make an educational video on AIDS with some of their kids. We accepted the project with the understanding that we would be gone for a week in July for our cruise. I love the challenge of writing and directing the video. I usually enjoy working with kids but those kids are going to be a tough bunch to motivate.

June 19, 1995

My stomach and digestive problems seem worse. I'm constantly popping over-the-counter medications for indigestion. Al thinks my problem has to do with the kids, but I don't think so. I know it's not good for me to jump up and down on feet that are already compromised with peripheral neuropathy (a tingling or pins-and-needles sensation much like you get when your hand or foot falls asleep). I just can't get these kids to respond to me. I'm not used to that. Maybe my frustration is contributing to my indigestion, who knows?

July 18, 1995

We almost missed the ship but we didn't and we had a great time on the cruise. What happened? Well, typical us, when we left Denver, we didn't leave enough time to clear international travel at the airport. At the airport we got into the wrong line. We finally got into the right line, but we never would've made our flight, if I hadn't caused such a scene. The actress in me kicked into high gear. I started to cry and plead with the people at the gate.

"If we miss our flight then we're going to miss our ship in Vancouver," I cried. People let us go to the head of the line. Later, Al smiled. He couldn't believe I pulled it off. Guess he forgot what a great actress I once-upon-a-time was.

We met my parents on the ship and told them the story. They laughed, too. Al said it wasn't funny at the time. He would never forget my great scene nor would he ever fly again without leaving ample time to make a flight.

I'm glad that we took the cruise. Dad had wanted to take the trip for years. I, too, thought it would be a great adventure and it was. Al and Mom, who were more reticent about the trip, had a fabulous time, too. I felt on top of the world when we sat on a glacier after our helicopter flight. The air in the Misty Fiords was so pure and pristine. In Glacier Bay we watched the glaciers calve. It was a beautiful sight.

Al and I even entered the ship's talent show. It felt awesome to step on a big stage again just to perform music. I really miss that part of my life. We won the talent contest. Guess we were ringers since we were probably the only professionals in the contest. It was wonderful seeing my parents relaxed and having so much fun. Just magical moments.

Since returning to Denver, we've been working on the Arapahoe House project. I've made it a game show called, Death B4 Time. Somehow, we managed to complete the project, tape the show and put it "in-the-can" the night before my BIG HIT!

Chapter Sixteen

THE BIG HIT
July-September 1995

July 18, 1995
I decided to put my name in the "Saquinavir lottery."
Let me explain. There was going to become available a pre-
cious small amount of the new promising HIV drug called
Saquinavir, which was the first of a brand new class of drugs
called protease inhibitors. The only way to get the drug
through Denver General was by lottery.

I called my folks to tell them that I had put my name
in the lottery. I never expected to win. I knew that my parents
would be pleased that at least I had tried to get one of the
newest drugs to treat HIV.

On August 18, 1995, a Friday afternoon, I learned
that I had won the lottery! For an AIDS patient Saquinavir
was like winning liquid gold. I knew that this drug wasn't a
cure. But all the research was so promising. A little piece of
me hated to believe that maybe, just maybe, I could still beat
this thing. A big piece of me was almost scared to believe it.

Later that evening, I vomited. This was not an un-
usual occurrence, but it happened again several times during
the night. The next morning Al tried to convince me to go to
the emergency room of Denver General. At first, I stubbornly
refused to go. But by evening, after being sick all day, I
agreed to go. The young doctor on duty said that he didn't
think there was anything wrong with me. He recommended

that I stay in the hospital for 24 hours for observation or he said I could go home. It was a mistake to give me a choice. I obviously opted to go home. I continued to vomit. By late Sunday afternoon, I was unbelievably sick. My nurse practitioner, Patty, stopped by our house. My heart rate was 180 and I was so dehydrated that she immediately took Al and me back to the hospital and stayed with us until I was admitted into a room. Patty literally saved my life. Al called my folks. I spoke with them briefly before I drifted off to sleep. I would wake up mostly just to throw up. I was in a lot of pain, so I slept very fitfully. I told Al to go home and get some sleep, but he wouldn't leave my bedside.

The next morning I awoke and saw a doctor standing by my bed. He said that I had pancreatitis. (Later, Al learned that what impacted my pancreas was lactic acidosis, a side effect from D4T). He then asked me if I wanted to activate my DNR (do not resuscitate). I told him "no."

"Okay. Then I'm going to take you into the Intensive Care Unit and sedate you. We will flood your body with fluids to see if we can get your pancreas to function normally."

I wasn't sure what was going to happen to me next. I called Mom. "They're taking me into the ICU," I tried to remain calm to allay some of her fears, but I was very scared.

Mom said that she'd get on the next plane to Denver. I told her to wait until she spoke with Al. He was downstairs at the Denver General McDonald's getting a cup of coffee. Everything was happening so fast. I didn't care what they did to me because I was in so much pain. I was quickly sedated. There is little or nothing that I can tell you about the next 11 days of my life. I was given drugs to erase my memory. Believe me those drugs just wiped those days away. It was as if someone had hit a delete button on the computer of my life. They are just gone.

I had spoken with Dee Dee on Friday, Saturday and Sunday so I knew that she was sick but I had no idea how sick. On Monday morning, when she called and told me she was in the hospital and that the doctors were moving her into ICU, my heart leaped into my throat. I grabbed my suitcase, which was always half-packed, and threw a few more things into it. I was planning to fly to Denver in a few days as part of my ritual of regular trips so I already had a ticket. I called my travel agent to find out which flights on Monday had open seats. Al called me and said that Dee Dee needed the ICU to help her breathe. He said that her doctors were gravely concerned about her blood gasses. I told him that I would be on the 4:30 p.m. flight to Denver. I left my house at 3 p.m. and arrived in Denver around 9 p.m. (Mountain Time). Al met me at the airport and we rushed straight to the hospital.

I remember glancing at the clock in the hall in the hospital. It was 9:45 p.m. Al and I quickly walked to the end of the darkened hallway on the 11th floor in Denver General. A young woman, the pulmonary resident on duty, met us at the doorway of the ICU. We sat on two old card chairs in the dimly lit hall. She gave us a full report. It was very bleak. Al and I looked at each other with pure terror on our faces.

"If she survives the night, it will be a good sign but no promises," she said to us.

We looked for a place to spend the night at the hospital. The tiny closet of a space that they called the ICU waiting room had two vinyl chairs and a two-seater couch, a TV set and a pay phone on the wall. The doctor encouraged us to return to Dee Dee and Al's home. It was only seven minutes from the hospital. She reassured us that she would call us if there were any change in her condition.

"This could be a very long haul," she said. "My advice to you two is to go home and get a good night's sleep. We promise to call you if anything happens."

We went home but if the doctor thought that either of us was going to get much sleep, she was wrong. We were both

149

too afraid to fall asleep. We feared that the phone would ring and the hospital would say that Dee Dee had died, though neither of us could express that fear in so many words.

I called Howard at midnight. "You better get on the first flight in the morning to Denver. I don't know if Dee Dee is going to make it." Howard had no idea that our daughter's condition was that grave and he was sorry that he had sent me ahead of him. "Are you alright?"

"No, but Al and I are hanging on to each other. We'll be okay. You just get here as fast as you can."

"I will, honey. I will." Howard promised.

Now none of us would get a decent night's sleep. I could have called Howard in the morning. He could not get on a flight until then, anyway. Once again, I was just running on raw emotions. All rational thinking just evaporated.

Al and I sat on his living room couch and talked into the wee hours of the morning. Al said there was no way that he would still be alive if this happened to him. He said his age and his heart would never withstand what Dee Dee already had. I became painfully aware of how he must feel being infected with the same virus and watching these events unfold before his eyes. Eventually exhaustion prevailed upon both of us. I fell asleep on the couch. Al fell asleep on the living room floor. I perched one portable phone two inches from my ears. Al had their other portable phone two inches from his head.

By 5 a.m. we were sitting in the kitchen drinking very strong coffee. No phone calls during the night thank God. At least she had survived the night. By 7 a.m. we were showered, dressed and back at the hospital. During the previous evening Howard finally connected with Alan who had been on a business trip. Alan got home around 1 a.m.

"Son, I need you to meet me at the airport first thing tomorrow morning. Dee Dee is gravely ill. She's in the Intensive Care Unit in Denver General," Howard told Alan.

"Sure Dad, I'll be there."

By 9:30 a.m. both Alan and Howard came into my view as they navigated the corridor of Denver General to the ICU. I ran into my husband's arms.

"Is she alive? Do I have a daughter?" he implored.

"Yes, come," I said, "we can go see her."

"I can't, Mom," Alan begged off. "I just can't see my sister that way. I'll be back with Denise later."

"I understand son," I told Alan. "Thanks for meeting Dad at the airport and bringing him here."

Howard came with me into the ICU. Dee Dee was an unbelievable sight. Tubes and wires covered every part of her body. She was on a ventilator and she was hooked up to numerous monitors. Fluids were being flushed through her body and her little body had begun to swell. It was a surreal scene and frightening beyond words of description.

Later that afternoon, Al and Dee Dee's friend, a Unity minister, arrived. She showed us how to be with our daughter and how to talk to her and hold her through all those tubes. She helped us get past all the scary equipment. It was so painful to watch Dee Dee struggle to breathe on the ventilator.

Early that evening, Al set his telephone trees in motion. Visitors, all of Dee Dee and Al's friends started to flood the hospital and the ICU waiting room—Lucy, Debbie, Craig, and Sami. Dear Sami, dragging her own portable oxygen tank she affectionately named Stuart, came to the hospital every day. Sami's lungs were so crippled with arthritis that she was on a transplant list waiting for a new lung, but she never missed a day. She brought a new bag of goodies for us daily. Jody, Dr. Cohen, Dr. Judy, Patty, Dr. Morrie and Dr. Mallore continued to visit. Jews, Christians, Buddhists and Catholics said prayers. Jewish prayers were said for healing and masses were held in New Orleans, Austin and Detroit. Prayers were even offered at the Partridge Family Temple and the Pillar of the Flame, all for my daughter who was clinging to life on a spider web's thread.

I was so anxious. I tried taking tranquilizers but they made me feel tired. I needed my energy and strength so I abandoned them. The constant parade of friends gave me moments of relief from the pure terror I felt. I was not ready for Dee Dee to die. Would I ever be?

Patrick caught a flight to Denver from Texas and spent every day at the hospital with Dee Dee and us. Bud came to the hospital on several occasions. Then Doug and his dad came to see Dee Dee. So many people loved her. Could love and prayers sustain her? We hoped that it would.

First good news: a CAT scan showed a little less swelling of Dee Dee's pancreas. Her condition was changed from critical to stable. I exhaled a little. She was beginning to heal. My daughter, my tough little steely lady was fighting for her life. More flushing. Her body continued to swell. We laughed as she began to look like the Pillsbury doughboy. Our skinny Dee Dee was all puffed out.

The next day we continued our watch. More visitors came—Al's sister, Nina, and my brother, Dee Dee's Uncle Joe. Phone calls came in from all over the country. Greg, Mark, Randy, Janey, Katie, Cindy and Virgil came by to visit. Jay and Bud returned to the hospital, again and again. How had she impacted all of these people in the relatively short time that she had lived in Denver?

It was August 25, 1995. We continued our vigil by our daughter's bedside. Thank goodness, the ICU was open to the constant stream of visitors. Howard stood at the foot of our daughter's bed every moment. He learned how to read her charts so well that an intern asked him if he was a doctor.

Today was going to be a big day, or so we thought. The effort began to awaken Dee Dee. We all tried to reach her. First Patrick tried to arouse her, "Dee Dee, Jana is sick and you need to go on." He tried to make her think that she was needed on stage. She would not awaken from her slumber. Nothing appeared to stir her. Al, Patrick, Howard, Bud and I kept trying. We had no luck. Then Sami visited and affixed a little guardian angel to one of Dee Dee's IV poles.

Later that day, Debbie and Sue arranged for us to be their guests for dinner at a restaurant across the street from the hospital. Food. I ate because Howard insisted that I eat to keep up my strength. Everything tasted like rubber to me. My only hunger was for my daughter's health. There was nothing more devastating to me than to not be able to make things better for my child. But I appreciated Debbie and Sue's offer of sustenance and outstretched arms of love they gave to us.

My brother, Joe, came back to Denver and went straight to the hospital. Marie and her boyfriend made their plans to fly to Denver from New York. Everyone offered to help. People offered to give blood. Shawn Marie stopped by to say hello. People called constantly, Katie, Dave, Don, Craig, Lon, Kathy, Ted and Christine. Dee Dee had touched so many people. I watched all her friends flock around her. As the noted Jewish philosopher, Elie Wiesel, wrote, "For me friendship has always been a necessity, an obsession. Friendship or death, the Talmud says. Without friends existence is empty, sterile, pointless. In a man's life friendship is even more than love...." How richly blessed my daughter was to have so many friends.

On August 26 Howard, Al and I arrived at the hospital at 7:30 a.m. We hoped that the doctors would remove the ventilator. But we discovered that Dee Dee ran a fever during the night. Her doctors decided that they needed to pin down the infection before they removed her breathing tube. While this was disappointing news, we saw Dee Dee awake for the first time in nine days and better yet, she recognized us. We had her back! But she was in pain. Every pain she felt cut like a knife through my heart. I wanted to help her but there was nothing I could do. Dee Dee was feisty. Were we holding her here? Was it fair? I could not let her go—not yet. She could have let go, but she did not. This was a tough day. We were able to talk to a conscious Dee Dee, which was the good news; the bad news was she communicated her pain to us.

It was August 27 and a Sunday. We learned that unfortunately nothing changes in the ICU on Sundays so the doctor kept Dee Dee on the ventilator. We encouraged Al to go to his job, which was playing piano for a church. Howard, Patrick and I took turns sitting beside Dee Dee's bed. Sweet Patrick. He was such a big help. This is when he redeemed himself in my eyes. Dee Dee was so comforted by his presence. Finally, I came to appreciate the young, gay man who broke Dee Dee's heart in college. He and Dee Dee had a mature friendship, a special bond like the special love between a brother and a sister.

Marie called from New York to tell us that she had been in a minor car accident, but she was determined to come to Denver on Wednesday even if she had to be on crutches or if she needed a wheelchair to get around.

Dee Dee still had a fever. Her doctors continued to test her to look for the source of the infection. We decided not to allow visitors that day except for Alan and Denise who drove to Denver from Boulder to visit with her.

Around noon, the tech started Dee Dee breathing on her own leaving the tube in her throat. Al arrived after work and he was elated to see that Dee Dee could shake her head in response to his questions. He asked her if she was in pain. She shook her head from side to side indicating no. He asked her if she wanted the tube removed. Her eyes flared real wide and she shook her head yes. Al told her that he felt certain that tomorrow they would remove the tube. Even though the tube remained in her mouth, she was for the most part breathing on her own and it was beautiful just to watch her breath and rest quietly. It was wonderful to have Dee Dee back with us and not see her writhing in pain. Our rabbi from Dallas called to send his love and prayers. Then, Craig, Sami and Nina came by to visit again.

The next day the breathing tube was removed. Her blood chemistry improved every day. Dee Dee asked to go home. She wanted the oxygen mask removed from her face. She was breathing on her own. The mask was for misting her throat, which was terribly dry. It scared Dee Dee to be voiceless. The nurses sat Dee Dee up in a chair for a few minutes but she was so uncomfortable that she asked to be put back in bed. More visitors came by. I told her that I was going back to her house. Sami had arranged for her hairdresser to come by the house to give me a haircut. Dee Dee smiled. She knew that life was returning to normal if I was going to get a haircut. Funny, how the ordinary acts of life become so significant to someone who is sick.

Alan visited again. He was thrilled to see his sister so alert. I told Dee Dee that Howard would have to return to Dallas the next day and I was considering a trip back to Dallas by the end of the week. Dee Dee seemed pleased. She never said, "Don't go," to me. With all the treks we took between Denver and Dallas, never once did I hear Dee Dee complain when we said we had to leave Denver. She was still a very sick girl, but at least she was on the road to recovery.

Greg and Shawn Marie stopped by the hospital to visit the next day. Dee Dee was improved but still having trouble with nausea. Her pancreas settled down but was still not right. It hurt me when I overheard Dee Dee tell Shawn Marie to take care of Al. It sounded like she did not expect to be a wife to Al much longer. Tears touched my eyes. Sick as Dee Dee was she worried about Al. Dee Dee fell asleep. Jay stopped by. He told us not to wake her. He stood by the foot of her bed and just smiled. He looked at us and softly said, "Miracles do happen." We agreed.

When Dee Dee woke up, Howard told her that he planned to return to Dallas the next morning. "Go, Daddy. I know that you need to return to work," she weakly replied.

It was a rough night. Dee Dee was miserable. She was nauseated again and going through medication withdrawal. She was most uncomfortable. Al was extremely concerned.

The next morning, the doctors changed Dee Dee's anti-nausea medication and she appeared to feel a little more comfortable. My sides hurt every time I saw her dry heave. She tried to force down a liquid diet. At noon, Patrick told her that he had to return to school. "Bummer," she said to him, "I missed most of your visit because I was knocked out. It just isn't fair." She managed a tiny smile.

He gently stroked her forehead and promised to return for a visit later when she felt better. He then kissed her good-bye. I decided that for Dee Dee's 27th birthday in September, we would purchase a ticket and fly Patrick back to Denver so that they could have a real visit. Dee Dee dozed off. Al drove Patrick to the airport and dropped him off at his terminal. He waited at the airport to meet Marie and her boyfriend, Gary.

When Al returned to the hospital with them, Dee Dee brightened up.

"Hi, Marie. You look cute. Know what Marie? I finally had something that you never had, pancreatitis." The two sick girls laughed. It never occurred to us that Marie was feigning the illnesses and procedures that she described in great detail to Dee Dee and others.

August 31, 1995

When I woke up in the ICU, Dr. Cohen told me that I had the worse case of pancreatitis he had ever seen. He quickly added that he had given me drugs to erase my memory of the whole experience. I felt frustrated because I didn't know what had happened to me. Mom kidded Dr. Cohen. She asked him if she and Al could have some of those drugs! Poor Mom and Al, they look so tired. I'm really worried about Al. Mom at least has Dad but whom does Al have? I loved seeing Patrick, but most of the time that he was here I was knocked out. It's not fair.

Marie and I had to communicate by writing notes to each other because neither one of us had a voice. Mine was still very raspy from the breathing tube. Marie told us that she had lost her voice from radiation treatments on her throat cancer. The two of us, the original chatterboxes—silenced. Strange.

I'm scared. They want me to move into a regular room. I don't want to leave the ICU. Everyone else is happy about it except for me. Marie said this is a positive step. It's just that in the ICU I get so much attention. There is one nurse for every two beds. Out there on the floor there is one nurse for the whole floor. Mom, Marie and Al promise to never leave me alone in my room. Mom said that she would hire a practical nurse to spend the night if I needed it. My fears settled down a bit after I moved to a bed on the floor.

September 1, 1995

Where did August go? Oh yeah, those memory drugs. Today I had a rough time of it. The docs wanted to be sure that my lungs were clear. So this morning they took me to the radiology department and gave me a chest X-ray and a sonogram. They removed some fluid from my lungs and then gave me another X-ray. I'm so pooped from all the procedures. Later today they are going to remove my catheter. I'm running another fever. It's 102 but at least I can rest. Tiff, one of my friends from Arts, flew in from New York yesterday and stayed with me until 3 a.m. I loved her visit. She was really a terrific nurse.

September 2, 1995

They moved me again, this time from a four-bed room to a two-bed room with no one in the second bed. I wonder if that is because I have AIDS. I slept much better. Marie and Gary have to return to New York today. Maybe if I don't wake up they won't go. Marie and I had a good cry last night. She promised to return to Denver as soon as possible. Tiff is still here but she leaves tomorrow. I'm mostly bedridden and pretty content to sleep.

September 3, 1995

Mom gave Al the day off today. She told him to go home and get some sleep. So what does my crazy husband do? He cleans the house and cuts the grass. He says that is his way of relaxing. Then he took a short nap.

A nurse gave me a tub bath and shampoo a little while ago. I didn't like sitting in that cold tub. But afterwards, it felt great to be bathed and cleaned. Denise and Alan came by for a short visit. They brought Ben. I didn't want my nephew to see me this way. I'm afraid it will scare him, so when he was here I played hide and seek under my covers. It was good to hear him giggle. I love that gorgeous little boy. Mary came by for a visit, too. After a brief chat with her, I told her that I needed to rest. Mom said I was always good about letting my visitors know just how much visiting I could tolerate and when it was time to go.

157

After my nap, Patty stopped by. She got me out of my bed and walked me to the door of the room and then back to my bed. I'm so weak but my Mom's smile made the walk worthwhile. Al arrived and Mom went back to our house and left us alone for a visit. They've hired a practical nurse to stay with me during the night. I just feel so needy at night.

September 4 was Labor Day. Dee Dee was awake when I arrived in her room. She had another rough night because she spiked another fever. Thank goodness the fever broke by morning. She was still slightly nauseous but that calmed down enough for her to take her pills again. She was living on a steady diet of Popsicles and Snapple tea. Dee Dee was sitting up watching the Jerry Lewis Muscular Dystrophy telethon when I arrived.

"Hi, Mom. Could you do me a favor? Please make a donation to Jerry's kids for me."

"Sure, honey." My heart swelled. Here she was in a hospital bed sick from complications of AIDS and she wanted to do something for Jerry's kids. Then Dee Dee tried to hum a few notes. Her voice cracked and it annoyed her.

"Dee Dee, I'm thinking about going back to Dallas for a couple of days. If I do, then Daddy and I will return to Denver next Saturday. What do you think?"

"Hey, Mom, that's fine. Maybe by Saturday I'll be out of the hospital and back home."

"I hope so." I gave her a big hug.

Her doctors had reduced her dose of morphine and they were pleased that she was doing okay on the smaller dosage. She still felt puny most of the time. It did not help that she ran a fever and was uncomfortable from the slight nausea as well as the constant elimination of all the fluids that had been flushed through her body. But her worst complaint was the pain in her feet and legs, which were swollen from periph-eral neuropathy (a condition that effects the nerves in the body's extremities and one of the side effects of many HIV medications).

Al met Dr. Morrie on one of his breaks outside of the hospital. He told Al that Dee Dee had taken a major hit, as if we did not notice. But what was most disturbing was his next statement. "Don't expect her to come back to the level of functioning that she had before the pancreatitis."

I know that Al and I were not willing to accept the full impact of the doctor's words. It was recommended that we find an acute care unit for Dee Dee when she was discharged from the hospital. Al and I went to visit one of those facilities. We decided against putting Dee Dee in one of those places. Al said that he would turn their house into a critical care unit and that is exactly what he did. He removed the shower doors from their tub and affixed safety bars around the tub. We bought a shower seat so she could sit in the tub and he installed a hand-held showerhead. He ordered a special raised toilet seat with handles, a walker and a wheelchair. Thus began the conversion of their home into a critical care unit.

On Monday, September 11, Dee Dee told Al to get her a wheelchair. She wanted to appear at the Colorado AIDS Walk! "I promised that I would be there this year if last year's walkers returned," Dee Dee said. Al pleaded with her not to go but she insisted. Al arranged for Jay to bring his van and they borrowed a wheelchair from the hospital. The first time I saw Dee Dee attempt to smile after her ordeal was at the Walk. There was a huge crowd of 14,000 walkers. Al sang "Somewhere Over the Rainbow" for the both of them. She gave him the thumbs up sign. A newspaper reporter snapped her picture. There are days when I wish I did not have that newspaper clipping. She looked so bad. Her eyes were sunken and black and her hair was all matted and flat. But I am glad that I have the picture because it reminds me of her bravery and lack of self-concern when it came to her work for AIDS. Whenever I feel discouraged, I look at that newspaper clipping and it inspires me to keep marching forward.

Later, that evening, Dr. Judy returned from her vacation and stopped by the hospital to visit Dee Dee. "Dee Dee," she said, "if you don't get out of that bed right now, you will spend the rest of your days bedridden." That was all my daughter had to hear.

Chapter Seventeen

THE FINAL CURTAIN
September 1995-June 27, 1996

In mid-September, I took the first of many brief four-day weekends in Dallas. I was always torn between being in Denver with Dee Dee and my home in Dallas. Once home, I unpacked and repacked some clothes, paid a few bills, spoke with a few friends and saw my counselor before returning to my daughter's side in Denver. It was a short but necessary break for me. Even though I was physically removed from the Colorado scene for a few days, I could never remove myself emotionally from it.

When I returned to Denver, Dee Dee had been home from the hospital one day. I could not wait to see her. Al retrieved me from the airport and brought me to their house. I walked straight into her bedroom. She was lying there asleep. Pale, thin, and so still she looked like a corpse. I left the room quickly to cry. Dee Dee woke up and called to me.

"Mom? Is that you? Come here." She took my face into her bony little hands and looked me straight in the eyes and said, "Mom, I'm going to be fine. Please don't cry." My daughter never wanted any of us to be sad. I saved my tears for when I was alone at bedtime.

A few days later, Dee Dee developed the worst possible complication, a pseudo-cyst on her pancreas. The nausea and pain returned. She was bedfast once again. About four weeks later, her doctor put in a drain to alleviate the cyst and to hopefully inflate her stomach. She began to eat and gradually was able to process some food.

When I returned to Dallas, Al and Dee Dee's dear friend, Darryl (the drummer from the *Cinderella* tour) flew to Denver from Detroit to be with them. I affectionately called Darryl my black angel and he called me his Jewish mother. My daughter especially enjoyed Darryl's quiet, caring demeanor. Al appreciated his help, too, and I always felt relieved to know that whenever I could not be in Denver, Darryl was there. Darryl and Al forged a close friendship after being the "band" from the *Cinderella* tour for nine months. His apparent sisterly love for Dee Dee flowed from his caring heart.

It was November 20 when Dee Dee's doctors finally removed the tube and bag from her cyst. We were all relieved. She was looking forward to celebrating Thanksgiving Day at Alan and Denise's home. It would be her first real outing since the AIDS Walk in September.

She handled the car trip up the mountain to their home well and she enjoyed being with the family. Dee Dee especially loved holding her nephew Ben in her lap and reading him a story. Even if she looked like a concentration camp survivor, there was always her irrepressible smile and sparkling eyes. I masked my pain. The next day Dee Dee needed to stay in bed all day just to recuperate from her little pleasure trip.

After 24 hours of bed rest, Dee Dee recovered. She got out of bed, walked to the bathroom, brushed her teeth and then walked to the kitchen to eat. For Dee Dee this was a major accomplishment. I became painfully aware of her struggle to just do the ordinary tasks of living.

Al was doing okay. His role as her primary caregiver and the sole person to take care of their house and the rest of their life never overwhelmed him. He even worked part-time throughout this entire ordeal. We helped them financially as much as we could. Whenever I visited, I took over the kitchen, ran errands, did laundry and so forth. Though Al's burden was monumental, I never heard him complain. In fact, he always said it was his honor to be her caregiver.

I stayed for 10 days during that Thanksgiving visit and upon my daughter's request, cooked all of her favorite Jewish foods, like brisket, noodle kugel, and stuffed cabbage. She ate some of it. I was hopeful that maybe—just maybe, she would begin to regain some of the weight that she had lost. But it never did come back.

I was exhausted from all the traveling but I had no choice. I played the hand I was dealt. My next scheduled trip to Denver was planned for mid-December.

Shortly after I returned home, Marie called Dee Dee. She begged Dee Dee to meet her in Dallas for Christmas. Marie said that her heart was weak from her chemo treatments and her doctor would not allow her to travel to the mile-high city of Denver. It was okay for her to travel to Dallas so she planned to spend Christmas with her family.

Dee Dee called to tell me that she and Al wanted to come to Dallas for Christmas. Surprised and worried, I told her I did not think she should do the trip. Dee Dee still required IVs at night. She was very weak and compromised. The last thing I felt that she needed was to fly to Dallas at holiday time with all the holiday travelers. Howard and I discussed the trip at length. Neither of us had the heart to say that she could not come home. I guess deep in my soul, I did not believe that either Marie or Dee Dee would live to celebrate another Christmas, so we relented and sent tickets to Denver for Al and Dee Dee to fly home for the holiday.

December 20, 1995

I'm looking forward to celebrating Christmas with Marie's family. Al packed our suitcases last night. I know that I'm probably too weak to travel, but it hasn't stopped me before and I won't let it stop me now. Al suggested that I wear a surgical mask on the plane to protect me from germs. I told him, "No way." Besides, I don't seem to catch ordinary germs. I can't remember the last time I had a cold, probably because I'm so pumped up with antibiotics. I'm not happy

162

about traveling in a wheelchair, but I know that I am not strong enough to walk the distances in the airports.

December 24, 1995

We arrived in Dallas. Mom and Dad met us in the airport. I could tell from the expressions on their faces that they were worried about me. I barely had enough energy to welcome them with my smile.

December 27, 1995

Mom bought me this cute little denim Christmas blouse to wear on Christmas Day, a major concession on her part since I don't think she ever wanted to acknowledge my celebration of Christmas. I loved being with Marie, and Tiff was home for the holidays, too. I got to play Jewish Santa at Marie's home on Christmas morning even though the volume of gifts outweighed my energy to distribute them. I didn't have the strength to do very much with my friends, but the time we spent together was the best. I loved being with my girlfriends. For just a few special moments, I could feel like a 27-year-old girl again.

January 10, 1996

I saw Dr. Judy today. We sat and talked at great length about my meds. She explained, "I have your Saquinavir, but I'll be honest with you, Dee Dee, I'm afraid to give it to you. It's so new and we don't have any real track record on its effectiveness. It's very promising but you need to know that one of the possible side effects of this drug is pancreatitis." I told her, "no thank-you."

While many AIDS patients in 1996 were snatched from the jaws of death with the new protease inhibitor drugs, it was the second one, Crixivan, that provided the magic bullet in some, but not all the cases. The first generation of Saquinavir proved ineffective and has since been reformulated. Today everyone has heard about all the wonderful new treatments for AIDS. What they may not know is that of the population of people who are privileged enough to afford them, about one-third receive no benefit and no one is sure why. Another one-third cannot tolerate the drugs and discontinue taking them because of the side affects, and the other one-third benefits greatly. Many AIDS patients got a second lease on life in 1996 and the death rate dropped dramatically. Dee Dee was terribly compromised when she was offered the first protease inhibitor. Given what is known today about that drug, her decision not to do it probably was a good one.

Dee Dee called me shortly after her appointment with Judy. "Guess what Mom? I saw Judy today. She actually still has my Saquinavir and offered it to me, but one of the possible side effects is pancreatitis. I just can't do it, Mom."

"I understand, Dee Dee." I had to understand. This was her life and her decision. Was I disappointed? Certainly I was. Would it have made a difference? Most likely, no.

February 10, 1996

A producer from the Sally Jessey Raphael show called yesterday. They are doing a program on AIDS and want Al and me to come to Chicago to do it. Wow, my first chance to do national TV! I called Alan, who has lots of media experience and asked him what I should do. He advised me to wait until "Oprah" calls or to do the Sally show only if the show's producer is willing to come to Denver for the taping. I desperately want to tell my story on national television but I'll listen to Alan. I'll have Al call the producer and tell her no.

Dee Dee told me about the TV show. She seriously considered doing it. I could not believe her. I looked at her and wondered, "How did she think she had the strength to do something like that?" She was, for the most part, bedfast.

January through March I traveled back and forth to Denver. I sat beside my daughter's bed and helplessly watched her decline.

"Dee Dee?"

"Yes, Mom?"

"I am thinking about some of the ridiculous fights we used to have when you were younger. I want your forgiveness for anything I have said or done that might have hurt you. I want you to know that I forgive you for anything that you have said that hurt me. I'm so proud of you and our relationship today."

"I know, Mom."

"I know you know but I need you to hear it from me."

"Okay, Mom. I love you."

"Me, too."

Oh how powerless I felt, as day after day, all I could do was continue my death vigil by my daughter's bedside. I couldn't concentrate well enough to read much even during Dee Dee's naps, but one day I picked up a book of poetry from her nightstand. Someone must have given the book to her or Al as a gift. In it was a poem by Jane Browell that she had written about her mother who was dying from cancer. I renamed it a "Mother's Lament," adapted it to this situation and recorded it in my journal.

> My daughter, you are so sick and frail,
> I cannot make you warm;
> I cannot guide you back to health
> Or shield you from all harm.
> My hands can touch but not heal,
> My arms can't hold or cure;
> What use my empathy while you
> Must struggle to endure?
> I cannot breathe to save your breath,
> And pain cannot be shared.
> What have I ever given you?
> To show how much I cared?
> Only a hope…a mother's love;
> A kiss…a special prayer.
> So much, no more I offer you
> 'Tis all I can or dare.

We hired a private duty nurse to work part-time to give Al some relief in the evenings. Kathleen was patient and kind with Dee Dee without being patronizing. So was our Visiting Nurses Association nurse, Mel. Dee Dee had a special bond with her caregivers and was always appreciative of the comfort they brought to her life.

April 3, 1996

Mom prepared a Passover dinner in my house. I had asked her to do it because I wanted my nephew to have his first seder in Aunt Dee Dee's home. All week long, I enjoyed tasting all the special foods as Mom prepared them for this ceremonial meal. I knew I had given her a big challenge. She mailed some of the packaged food to our house from Dallas before she arrived because she knew she would never find them in our neighborhood grocery stores.

The night of the seder was really weird. Al helped me dress in a little outfit that Mom bought for me in Dallas. I noticed that the size of the jumper was a girl's size 12. God, had I shrunk that much? With some help from Al and all the energy I could muster, I got dressed. It turned out to be the last time I got dressed or for that matter came to the table to eat. In the afternoon, I started to have spasms. I was twitching so much that Dad ran the fastest seder he ever did, and he was known for his speedy seders. When Kathleen arrived, she took one look at me and rushed me to the hospital. My sugar had shot way up again and I was having a major diabetic incident. The doctors stabilized me. Dr. Judy wanted to put a feeding tube in my chest.

I said absolutely not. She got angry with me. She said that she couldn't do anything more for me except to keep me comfortable. She was so sad. Me, I was just tired of it all, and I couldn't bear the thought of a tube in my chest. It didn't matter to me anymore and I told her that I'm okay with it.

Later that same evening, Mom got a call from Grandpa in Chicago. Grandma had taken a very serious fall. She was in an Intensive Care Unit in a hospital in Chicago.

So after Mom and Dad visited with me in the Denver General Intensive Care Unit, they caught a plane to Chicago.

When I arrived in Chicago, I went directly to the hospital. My mother was totally out of it. She had an inoperable blood clot on her brain and the doctors were making no predictions about her recovery. All I could do was be there for my dad who appeared to be relatively calm and rational considering the circumstances. I met with my brother the next day and clearly told him that my plate was obviously filled to overflowing just dealing with Dee Dee. I solicited his support to help Dad deal with this crisis with our mother. He told me he would do whatever he could to help, which gave me great peace of mind. Within two days I was back on an airplane to Denver to return to Dee Dee.

April 5, 1996
Two days later, Al took me back into the ICU and called my folks in Chicago. They left Chicago and flew back to Denver to be with me. Poor Mom, she looked totally wiped. How did she do it? My parents have a secret weapon. They are a team. They carry each other. Sometimes it's Mom's turn and sometimes it's Dad's turn. It's so beautiful. My Daddy loves her so much. I'm so lucky to have found that kind of love with Al. Guess we are just two very lucky ladies. Well, I survived that round in D.G., but I don't know how much longer I can keep holding on.

It was April 17 at 4 p.m. in Dallas when Al called to tell me the nurse gave Dee Dee 24 to 72 hours to live. I threw a few things into my suitcase and caught the next flight to Denver. I arrived in their home by 8:30 p.m. to find Dee Dee sitting up in bed, smoothing her covers. "Hi, Mom," she said, "I don't feel like it's my time yet."

"Then it isn't, darling," I replied heaving a huge sigh of relief.

She fell asleep. As I sat beside her my mind floated back to the scene in the hospital just two weeks earlier. I was with her when Judy begged Dee Dee to allow her to insert a feeding tube. Dee Dee stubbornly refused it. Judy, frustrated by her feelings of helplessness, sent Dee Dee home. Saddened, she told her there was nothing more she could do except to keep her comfortable.

Dee Dee told Al, "No more hospitals!" She did not want to die in a hospital bed. I watched Dee Dee struggle to live her last days of her life on *her* terms. I wondered from what well she drew her strength and courage. Mine was slipping away. She had reached the point all AIDS patients reach, when they are just too tired to continue the struggle to live. So I was not surprised when the call came because I knew that she could not hold on much longer—or could she?

It was April 18 and Dee Dee survived the first 24 hours. Marie flew to Denver from New York with Gary on two tickets we sent them. Marie was pale and thin. She said that she could only spend one day in Denver—her doctor's orders. I knew that Dee Dee would hold on if she knew that Marie was coming. I was terrified about what would happen when Marie had to end her visit.

Darryl decided to extend his visit. Howard, Darryl, Al and I divided up the tasks and time so we could best take care of Dee Dee. Kathleen continued to give us about 20 hours a week until she took ill and could no longer care for her.

Darryl and Al preferred doing the night shift. Howard and I did the day shift. For three days the four of us walked on eggshells. Seventy-two hours later—she was still with us.

"Guess the nurse was wrong," Dee Dee said to me. "Mom, I don't want to be taken to the hospital any more. If I stop breathing, please honor my DNR."

It was painful for me to hear her tell me her wishes. Yet I had to honor them. She slept more peacefully knowing that we would not rush her to the hospital any more. Then the doctors gave Dee Dee five to seven days to live because she was bleeding internally. To everyone's surprise the bleeding spontaneously stopped because we reached day eight and she was still alive and kicking. We all relaxed a bit. Our lives were lived in a weird state of suspended animation.

We just put one foot in front of the other and did what had to be done. What other choice did we have?

It was getting increasingly more difficult for me to just sit next by Dee Dee's bed. She was pale, bone thin, and so ill. When any of us could help Dee Dee with anything whether it was to bring her a bedpan or carry her to the port-a-potty or bring her a beverage or her pills, for that moment we felt useful in a totally impotent situation.

April 20, 1996

I woke up and asked Daddy to "dance" me over to my port-a-potty. I couldn't walk anymore so I put my feet on his and he gently held me upright. He slowly swirled me around the few steps from my bed to the port-a-potty. For a brief moment I was that little girl in my Mary Jane shoes and lacey anklet socks dancing with my Daddy for the first time.

By some miracle, Dee Dee stabilized after the bleeding incident. Her doctor then cancelled all her HIV meds except for Bactrim and Dylantin. It amazed me that we wrote voluminous notes and kept them in a three-ring binder notebook with all her vitals, pills and behavior each day. But my daughter kept the best track of her medications. Whenever I asked her how she did that she said, "I just do."

We gave Dee Dee pills to soothe her stomach, cough syrup for her cough, antihistamines to control her itching, and Megace to stimulate her appetite. There was pain meds and liquid morphine and with it all, she remained pretty lucid. Her sense of humor and her concern for us prevailed. Gradually her ability to express her emotions diminished. The most painful loss for me was when my daughter could no longer smile. Her wonderful smile robbed by AIDS!

"Dee Dee?" I never knew when I entered her room and her eyes were closed if she was asleep or....

"Yeah, Mom?"

"I just wanted you to know that I am here just like you have always been here for me. You have been the one person who encouraged me to grow in special ways. Remember when you encouraged me to go back to work?

"Yeah," Dee Dee softly replied.

"And when you sang *Mama A Rainbow* to me, how did you know that I was struggling with growing old?"

"I just love the words to the song, Mom."

All those days I kept busy cooking, grocery shopping, doing laundry and running myriad short errands. My biggest salvation was my daily journaling. Each day I would write, gathering the strands and pieces of the last three years of my life. I thought about Dee Dee's life. I thought about a quilt panel and what she would want it to look like when this was all over. She loved the quilt from the NAMES Project. What would symbolize her life? How hard Dee Dee fought to keep the show going on—her story—her song. Somehow I had to keep it going for her.

"Dee Dee? What's your favorite AIDS organization?"

"I don't know, Mom, if I have a favorite. I love the *NAMES Project* because the quilt speaks so beautifully to kids. I also like the work Elizabeth Glaser's *Pediatric AIDS Foundation* does for children with HIV. Guess there are so many good ones. It is hard for me to say which one is my favorite. Most helpful to me especially in the beginning was *Project Inform.*"

"I know. You rest now."

"Okay."

May 1, 1996

*Mostly I sleep. I keep the TV on. It's tuned to all the old sitcoms on Nick at Night—*I Love Lucy, The Honeymooners *and* The Carol Burnett Show. *Wow, they were such great comedic actresses. Would I have ever been the next Fanny Brice as a theater critic in Austin once wrote in his column about me? Guess I'll never know.*

I stare at the wall hanging Marie gave me for Christmas. It's navy blue, light blue and white and has two young angels ascending to heaven. One angel is leading the way. Is it Marie or I? Guess I've always led the way and Marie has followed me.

My Grandma is doing better, or so Mom tells me. I know that Grandma has an inoperable blood clot, but she survived the accident. I hope that my Grandma will be okay. She's a strong, feisty lady. If anyone can pull through it, Grandma, I know that you can.

Late April, while Howard and I were in Denver, we visited with our son and his family. Denise was expecting our second grandchild. In January when she and Alan knew that they were pregnant, the first person they told about the new baby was Dee Dee. Then they swore her to secrecy. She joked with them. "It's so hard to keep your secret. You better not do this to me again." In their hearts they prayed that their sister would be here to experience the birth of their second child in November.

We returned to Denver after a two-day visit with them. Dee Dee was peaceful and comfortable in her own bed. I thought, Dee Dee will die in her own bed on her own terms, when *she* is ready. I watched Howard crumbling before my eyes. I watched Al dissolve into tears. I had to hold it together. We all held each other together. We hugged. We wept. And, from time to time, we got on each other's nerves though we might have felt tired and frustrated, we never fussed at each other. We were Dee Dee's team of caregivers.

On May 2, a hospice nurse came to the house. I asked her if I had to release Dee Dee. Was she waiting for me to give her permission to die? She said that Dee Dee had the kind of personality that she would make that decision on her own and when she was ready, she would tell you.

"Dee Dee. It's Mom. Did you have a good night?"

"Yeah. I think so."

"Dee Dee. I want you to know how much I admire the strength and courage you have displayed throughout your life. You were so bold to walk away from your neighborhood junior high school to go downtown to high school at Arts and the determination it took for you to try-yet-again after every unsuccessful audition. You were so fearless going off to the University of Miami knowing no one and gutsy to leave the university but not quit college. What moxey you displayed by going to St. Ed's and the self-reliance you showed by moving to New York after college. It took *chutzpah* to sing in the cabarets in New York and steeliness to persist on the Cinderella tour when you were so sick."

"Oh, Mom, thanks for telling me that."

"Dee Dee, the bravest thing you ever did was after you were diagnosed with AIDS. You have lived your life to the fullest. I am so proud of how you have given of yourself to help others learn about AIDS. You've been a real hero."

"I don't know, Mom."

"Well, I do. Now rest, honey."

"Okay."

It was all so bizarre. Friends and family were constantly calling us. I kept writing and taking Patch, the dog, for daily walks. It relieved some of the tension. Howard struggled to run his business from long distance. Thank goodness for phones, faxes and express mail.

I asked one of my girlfriends to go into our house to collect some of our bills and the business checkbook and mail them to me so I could do the business payroll and pay our bills. Remember that this was supposedly a three-day trip. We were on day 15. I kept washing the same clothes. One day, I decided to go to the store and buy some more clothes. I ran out of my prescriptions. I called my doctor in Dallas who called our pharmacist who then mailed them to me. We were on a deathwatch and all the rest just did not matter.

Our nurse, Mel, told us that she had never seen anyone as loved as Dee Dee. She could not see how Dee Dee could hold on much longer. Dee Dee had a good day. Another friend from New York came for a visit. More beautiful flowers arrived from an aunt who cared.

Dee Dee was always a little ambivalent about flowers. She loved getting and looking at them but then she

172

would say that they reminded her of an impending funeral. We all had to laugh and she desperately wanted to see us smile.

On May 4, Dee Dee asked me, "When are you returning to Dallas?"

"I don' t know."

"Doesn't Daddy need to get back to work?"

"Not really," I fudged. "It's his slow time and he has a very competent staff taking caring of things."

"Oh, okay," she said as she drifted back to sleep.

Later that day she again asked Al when were we going home. I was not sure if she wanted us to leave so she could die or if she wanted us to leave so things in her home would appear normal again. Were we holding her here by our presence? If we left, would she let go or believe that she was okay? What should we do?

Later that evening, Howard and I privately discussed returning to Dallas. Howard said he would not go without me. I just could not leave my daughter's side. We decided to stay another week and then return to Dallas for only four days. I knew that the break would do us both some good. My husband needed to check in on his business and I could touch base with my life in Dallas. Besides, there is nothing so comforting as sleeping in your own bed.

On May 5 Mel stopped by the house. She checked Dee Dee's vitals and gave her another Epoetin injection. Mel and Dee Dee talked. Dee Dee had stabilized but she was very weak. She was just wasting away. She got out of the bed only to use the port-a-potty. Her spindly legs could barely support her body but she wanted to walk to the port-a-potty. We took turns supporting her. She barely had the energy to sit up long enough for us to change her nighttime tee shirt. So she did it herself. So little was left that she could do for herself. She still fed herself most of the time and took her medications—even asking for them by name. I was amazed that her mind could still track them. I placed the pills into her hand so she could look at them and take each one by herself.

She requested that I cook her some hot cereal. I fed it to her. She ate very little of it. Everything that she asked for she always preceded with a "please" and concluded with a "thank you." She never took our care for granted.

She rarely complained about pain. There were some low moans. Her feet and legs were the worst of it. Damn those HIV drugs and that awful side effect of the peripheral neuropathy. It crippled her. She hated it when her hands shook. I worried that the HIV would attack her brain and cause HIV dementia. What if I walked into her room one morning and she did not know who I was? I shuddered at the thought of it.

By May 6 Dee Dee was too weak to cough. She hated for anyone to be sad so I had to leave the room because I did not want to cry in front of her. Her friend Lucy stopped by for a visit. Dee Dee felt compelled to talk to her.

Later that evening, dinner was delivered from a local fast food restaurant. Several of my friends from Dallas got together and sent us dinner. They wanted me to know how much they cared. Al quipped, "Dinner for 40 just arrived." Not really. Kathleen was on duty that evening and the four of us sat down to eat dinner together, a rare event. Bless my friends from so far away. I knew if I was living through this nightmare in Dallas, my friends would have made this situation more bearable, but that was not how the stage had been set and we had no choice but to follow the design.

I never factored in how difficult it would be for my husband and me when Dee Dee decided to live in Denver. I longed to be home in my community of support. Yet, I doubt if Dee Dee took her dying journey in our home, if it would have truly been any easier. I concluded there is no good place for a Mom or a Dad to helplessly watch their child die.

On May 7 my brother was in Denver on business, so he came by the house to visit Dee Dee. He stood by her bed for a few minutes. Then he stepped outside of the front door of their home to draw in a few gulps of fresh air. He desperately wanted to suppress his emotions. He loved his niece and looking at Dee Dee in her deathbed was traumatic for him. He gathered his composure and insisted that Howard and I join him for some lunch at a nearby restaurant. I am not sure who needed whom more at that moment.

When we returned from lunch, the scene in the house was so surreal. Al was asleep upstairs. Dee Dee was asleep downstairs. Darryl quietly prepared to leave the house to run an errand. It was hard to believe that Dee Dee would soon be leaving all of us.

On May 9 I slept fitfully during the night but then why should that night be any different than the rest of them? I was terribly conflicted about leaving Denver. Dee Dee had a good night. She slept well even after the doctor lowered the dosage of morphine. Dr. Judy lowered it because Dee Dee complained about her shaky hands and feeling spacey. Mel visited and after her examination she suggested that we cancel our plans to leave because she didn't think that Dee Dee was stable. Howard and I talked about our trip once again. Should we go or should we stay? We decided that we absolutely needed to return home, if only for a couple of days. Darryl agreed to stay in Denver while we were gone and then he would go home when we came back to Denver.

May 11, 1996

Mom and Dad finally went home. I want to be alone with Al. So much is happening to me. I need to share it with him. I don't want him to fear the end. Ever since Dr. Judy and I talked in January, I realized that there's not going to be any cure for me. She promised to keep me comfortable and that she has done. Maybe, please God, there will be a cure for my Al, my love.

May 20, 1996

Al took a walk with his friend Aleene (not her real name). I became very nauseated and begged for my Inapsine shot. Al would give it to me when a nurse wasn't available, but this time Al was not home. Dad was the one who gave Alan and me our allergy shot when we were young because Mom couldn't do it. Dad came into the room grabbed a syringe and gave me my shot. Then he accidentally stuck himself when he tried to recap the syringe before he put the contaminated needle into the plastic disposable jug. Oh God, NO! Dad ran into the bathroom and washed his finger and drowned it in alcohol and peroxide. Mom just about lost it. What if Dad gets HIV? I just don't...Oh God...I hope not.

When Howard took his needle stick, he ran into the bathroom and cleansed the wound. I came into the bathroom and he told me what had happened. I nearly collapsed on the floor. I was afraid to scream out because I did not want to alarm Dee Dee. So I screamed inside myself. Howard said that he didn't think that Dee Dee knew what had happened. He was angry with himself for trying to recap the syringe. He did not realize that the contaminated syringes in the special disposable plastic container protected them. All he knew was that he did not want anyone else to come in contact with the contaminated needle.

Al returned to the house from his walk shortly thereafter and we told him what had happened. I ran upstairs and threw myself across our bed. "Oh, no, what if Howard got infected? How can I live through this one more time? When will this end?" I shut down at that point. I retreated into a world of silence, the silence that scares my family to death, and the silence that only those *infected* or profoundly *affected* by HIV know all too well. Both Howard and Al knew I had reached the end of my rope. They tiptoed around me.

We stupidly waited more than 24 hours before calling Dr. Judy (the optimum thing is to treat a needle stick within the first 24 hours). She ran an HIV test on Howard for a base line. Of course it was negative. If he were infected, the HIV antibodies would not show on the test for at least six weeks. She told Howard that he could opt to start on a course of AZT but he declined. She told him that he needed to be tested again in six weeks, three months and six months because 99 percent of all cases will appear within that period of time. She reminded us to use condoms. We knew Howard should retest anonymously. Dr. Judy then made this comment, "At least if you are infected, it happened while serving your daughter's needs." Some consolation, I thought.

On the ride home from the appointment, I was very quiet. Howard was more concerned about me than about himself. He said he wanted us to return to Dallas for another breather. "Alright." I begrudgingly agreed to leave Denver.

We arrived in Dallas on May 23. We decided not to tell anyone about the needle stick. No need to worry everyone else. Besides, all of our friends and family were dealing in their own way with Dee Dee's impending death. We did not see any reason to add to the burden.

After unpacking I retrieved my messages from my answering machine. There was a message from Dee Dee that surprised me since she had not initiated any phone calls in weeks. She simply said, "Sorry I missed your birthday, Mom." At the time I thought that Dee Dee had mixed up Mother's Day with my birthday. She did not exactly miss Mother's Day. We celebrated it in her room around her bed. I thought, "Maybe she had forgotten about our celebration, after all she was under some pretty heavy sedation drugs. Or maybe, just maybe, she knew that she would not be here for my birthday on July 3." I wondered if she would be here for Father's Day or Al's birthday on June 23. I shuddered to think about it.

We returned to Denver on May 27. I was amazed that Dee Dee was still clinging to life. When we separated the last time, I thought it might be our final goodbye. I thought if we left Denver that it was our tacit way of telling her it was okay for her to let go. Is she waiting for Al to release her?

She was thinner. Does she even weigh 60 pounds? Her movements were stiffer and appeared much more painful. She was so remote and her only expression of emotion was frustration or annoyance. Poor Al, he looked drained and grateful that we had returned to Denver so quickly. Where else would a mother be?

Dee Dee was withdrawn and detaching. For months we could barely touch her because she ached everywhere. She had not eaten anything for a couple of days and rejected all her meds except the ones for pain relief. If I thought that every day of our last visit was intense this was doubly so. We planned a two-week stay. Unless...*unless.* Each day I thought "this cannot get any worse," but it did.

I reached the point in my prayers where I asked God to take Dee Dee gently. Please do not make her suffer in the end. I knew when it was over it was over. All that would remain of our baby would be our memories. Our real daughter had left us months ago. Nothingness had been with us for what felt like forever. The sad irony of all of this was her whole life was about fun and bringing joy and laughter to our lives. Today my daughter looked like a withered old lady with virginal breasts. I thought to myself, "Death may soon silence your voice, Dee Dee, but it will not silence mine! Somehow, I will keep the lyrics of your song singing until this suffering is removed from the world."

On June 3 we could no longer put Dee Dee on a bedpan. It was too painful to move her, and even though she was in a waterbed, she had developed some nasty bedsores. Today we had to put her in diapers. Only flesh hung on her bony pelvis. It was such an irony that in all of Dee Dee's life, every time she viewed anything to do with the Holocaust, she would wince from the pain in her heart for her people. Now Dee Dee was a holocaust survivor herself—a different holocaust—the silent holocaust of our youth—AIDS.

Mel examined Dee Dee. Then she told Dee Dee that she would see her on Friday. Dee Dee replied, "Sometimes we're here and sometimes we're not."

On June 4 she was worse. Her lungs filled with fluid. We asked Mel, how much longer? "With Dee Dee, who knows?" She was one tenacious little person. Then Dee Dee vomited again. Al offered to give her another Inapsine shot. She refused it. She just wanted more morphine. How many weeks had it been since Dee Dee had been given one to three days to live?

"Oh God," I prayed, "when her time comes, let her die peacefully and not violently. May she have the ability to say what she wants to say before she dies. God, help my Mom to heal. Give Al many more good years. May the drugs finally get here to sustain his health. Are you listening, God? Please protect Howard from this horrific fate."

I talked to God a lot. I prayed for a healthy second grandchild and for a full recovery for my Mom and Marie. I promised God that I would devote the rest of my days to HIV-related work until the day there is a cure.

On June 6 Dee Dee said to Al, "It's time for us to go."

Al replied, "Who, Dee Dee? You and me?"

"Yeah."

Al said, "I will go with you as far as I can, but then you will have to go the rest of the way by yourself. And I will meet you there."

"Yeah. I'll go ahead. You meet me there."

The following morning I went into Dee Dee's room to take my place next to her bed. Her room was the final cocoon of her existence. As I entered, on the wall in front of me hung a picture with the words, "Follow your dreams for they are the hope of the future." Next to it was a cross-stitched Jewish Star. In the center of the star were three concentric circles sewn in blues, purples and pinks. It was a gift from Marie. To the right on another wall was a framed piece of music titled "Endless Love." It was a wedding gift.

The room was furnished with all the trappings of a terminally ill patient—a port-a-potty, a heating pad, a steam vaporizer and a nightstand display of Tylenol, a thermometer and lotions. Alongside her bed was a stack of waterproof pads for her to lie on, diapers and more powder, as well as a basket with a cover. Two bedpans were on the floor next to the basket and a variety of spit-up pans adorned other corners of her bed. On her dresser, which months ago became a "med cart," lay a stethoscope, a pediatric-sized cuff to take her blood pressure because her arms were so thin, and three large, sectioned plastic jars that held a variety of pills. Cough syrup, antihistamines, air freshener and a roll of toilet paper, as well as the red plastic container to properly dispose of used syringes, filled the top of the dresser. Next to her dresser was a laundry basket, neatly stacked with clean sheets and blankets.

Dee Dee's room reflected her life. Next to her bed was a large lounge chair for her guests—people were always very important to her. Her TV, VCR and a tape player delivered what little pleasures they could. A poem written by Sami adorned another wall. Over her bed was a picture of three little girls (who could easily be Dee Dee, Marie and Tiff) sitting on a wall surveying the ocean—the world their oyster that was not to be for her. Next to it, hanging on the wall, was a dream catcher—all her dreams that would not come true. In the corner was a wreath of hard candy that someone had given her. Directly across from Dee Dee's bed was this huge wall hanging of two angels ascending to heaven that Marie had given Dee Dee for Christmas. Next to it was a collage that Marie had made of pictures of all the people and happy events in her life. Marie sent it to her when she was in ICU last August. She loved it. Marie was the one friend in her life whom Dee Dee loved like a sister. On another wall was a plaque that Howard gave to Dee Dee. It read, "Dallas Cowboys' Biggest Fan." Some of the most special moments between Howard and Dee Dee were spent at a Cowboy football game when she was a little girl—Daddy's little girl.

Her small vanity table was adorned with an array of stuffed bunnies, bears and angels. Three hammocks chock full of stuffed animals were strung up in the corner echoing the free-spirited child that so reflected the woman she had become. On her other nightstand were pictures of Marie and Patrick, not to mention another angel and bear holding a heart and the small red beanbag bear that always accompanied my daughter to the doctor for her blood draws. Atop Al's dresser was a world globe that provided a soft night-light. It was a gift from her doctor. On her TV was a vase of fresh flowers. That was her world. That had been her world for months now; that would be her cocoon when she leaves this world.

"Good morning, sweetheart, Mommy loves you." I told her as I sat down beside her that morning.

"I love you too," Dee Dee softly replied, then drifted back to sleep. Her head was pointed toward the heavens. Her frail hand rested on her ashen face and sunken cheeks. She was quiet, so angelic looking.

Howard came into the room to relieve me. I was so sad and weepy. My chest physically hurt. Howard gave me a hug and suggested I take a break. He gave Dee Dee a massage with her favorite cocoa butter from the Body Shop. "Does that feel good, honey?" he asked her.

"Yeah," she replied.

I went outside the back door and sat on their deck to do some more writing. It was a beautiful spring day in Colorado. The sky was a clear blue. The sun felt warm and the air was cool. I heard birds chattering in the distance. The serenity was comforting. I wondered, "Is this how a soul prepares for death?"

Al returned from an errand at the post office. He sat on the deck with me for a few minutes. He joked with me that he was hard on his car, his clothes and his women. "No, Al," I thought to myself, "you are kind and gentle with your woman. Dee Dee has given this gift to you, to see yourself as a good, kind, gentle person."

The next day Dee Dee was alert. I told her that we would be spending the evening at Alan's home. I asked if she would like me to give him her love. "Of course, Mom."

"I love you, Dee Dee."

"I love you, too," she replied.

She was incredibly frail…just deadweight in
no muscle tone. Her skin hung wrinkled on her
huge eyes and long lashes lay across her wh

skull with skin. Her once beautiful thick hair was sparse and lifeless.

I was conflicted about leaving her even for a short visit with my son and his family in Boulder. What if she died while Howard and I were gone? I realized that her final act would be one that God and she would direct. She could die when I was asleep upstairs in her house or even when I was out doing the grocery shopping. Will it matter if I am not at her bedside when she dies? Will I be? Does she want me to be there? At that point I knew that I had to accept the final scene however it would be scripted.

Two days later we returned from Boulder somewhat rejuvenated. I enjoyed playing with my grandson Ben but I was more antsy than usual during my visit and glad to get back to Denver.

Dee Dee was awake and complaining about her legs. Al gave her some Amitryptaline. It gave her a little relief. She slept restlessly. She drank fluids but she had not eaten any solid food for two weeks. Today her lungs were clear, yesterday they were not.

Darryl called. He planned to return to Denver next week and said that he would stay through July 6. Howard and I discussed our plans. Exhausted and drained, we decided to return to Dallas when Darryl arrived.

Before we left, I asked Dee Dee if I could get her anything. "Yeah, Mom," she said, "a new life."

"I would if I could," I told her. "Dee Dee, I am so proud of you and how you have lived your life."

"Thanks, Mom."

"I love you, sweetheart."

"I love you, too, Mom.

I do not know why but when I kissed her goodbye, it felt final. We returned to Dallas on June 22.

It was June 26. Dee Dee awoke from one of her "turbo naps," as Darryl liked to call her deeper sleeps. She turned to Al and said, "I'm dying." Al responded, "Do you want to talk about it?" She softly whispered, "No. I just want to know."

On June 27 Dee Dee suddenly sat up in bed and said to Al, "I want to call my Daddy." This was unusual because she barely had the strength to talk to people when they called, rarely spoke on the phone and had not initiated any calls on her own in many weeks.

"I love you Daddy. Goodbye." she said to Howard in a barely audible voice.

Later that evening Howard told me that Dee Dee called him at work.

"Oh? I remarked with much surprise. "What did she say?"

"She just told me that she loved me and said good-bye. Her voice sounded so weak." Howard could no longer contain his tears. I held him tightly as he sobbed. I felt so sorry for him. In this one defining moment, Howard had finally come to accept a very difficult reality—his daughter was dying.

Chapter Eighteen

BEYOND THE FOOTLIGHTS
June 28, 1996

Friday, June 28 started for Al like many days had that spring and summer with all his thoughts on Dee Dee and her surviving yet another day. We all knew that her body was failing her, but day after day she surprised all of us with her determination to be around for one more day of life.

Just three nights before, Dee Dee sat up in bed and declared with great frustration, "Open the Gate! Open the Gate!" Al asked her what gate she was referring to and she pointed to the two large angels on the tapestry on their wall and said, "They won't open the gate. It's unlocked but they won't open it." Al suggested to her that maybe it was not her time to go through the gate.

Early in the morning on June 28 Dee Dee opened her eyes and asked Al to lie beside her and to hold her. It had been months since they had slept together or held each other. He delicately folded her little body into his arms and lay there for a few minutes. They told each other how much they loved each other. Al started to cry. "Please don't cry because if you do, I will and I'll never be able to stop," she said.

That evening one of Dee Dee's nurses, Nancy, was by her side and Darryl was upstairs resting. Al was in the back yard preparing the grill for dinner. Just before 9 p.m. Nancy came to the back door and said to Al, "I think you need to come quickly. I believe Dee Dee might be going."

Al raced up the stairs to get Darryl and they both were by Dee Dee's side in seconds. Darryl held her left hand

and Al held her right hand. Dee Dee lifted her head up a few inches. "What city?" she asked. Then a few seconds later she lay back down. "Oh, I see everyone now. Yes, I'll come with you. I guess I'll be going now. Okay, I'm going now."

First her breathing stopped and then a few minutes later her heart stopped beating. They lingered by her bedside telling her how much they loved her and then they wished her a safe voyage.

As the moment hung like butterfly wings, fragile and profound, they became aware of little sparkles glittering in the air around them. The three of them—Nancy, Darryl and Al saw it happening in the room where Dee Dee was and in no other. Every fifteen seconds or so a little rainbow oval formed. It would last for five seconds or so and then fade and reappear elsewhere in the room. This phenomenon continued for the next few hours.

Hours after her passing, Dee Dee's eyes continued to sparkle just like they had on that first night in Kansas when she and Al became a couple. Death could not rob her eyes of their special sparkle.

Dee Dee's indomitable spirit was dancing through the air, finally free of the earthly limitations of her body. She exited this life exactly as she had lived it—on her own terms, with grace and wisdom that defied her 27 years of living!

I had been given 39 months to prepare and Dee Dee had packed a whole lifetime of living into those months. I had the love of family and friends and the support of helpful professional people. Yet, when the call came from Al on that Friday evening, I realized that there was no preparation for the hole that was wrenched from my heart the evening my daughter Dee Dee died.

One year later.

After a brief welcome from the housemother, I began. "Hi. I'm Patti. Why am I here? I'm here tonight for one reason. That reason is my daughter, Dee Dee. She can't be here this evening, but if she were, this is what she would say."

DEE DEE'S STATEMENT
April 1996*

Hi. My name is Dee Dee Fields-McKittrick. I'm 27. I'm married. I'm Jewish. I'm a woman living with AIDS.

I grew up in Dallas, Texas in a very loving family. I fell in love with musical theatre when I was six years old. When I was in the eighth grade, I auditioned and was accepted into the Dallas Arts Magnet High School. In high school I didn't date a lot because I was so busy in shows or rehearsals. I was very shy about guys. While I always had a date for the B'nai Brith dances, most of my socializing with guys was done in groups.

After high school, I attended the University of Miami in Florida. While I was there I had an experience with a young man that until recently I just called a "really bad date." After therapy, I now know that it was an oral sex date rape. I was only 20 years old and didn't actually lose my virginity until I was 21. But that "bad date" shaped the way I handled my sexual relationships from then on.

I developed a fear and my fear kept me silent. The silence is what convinced me that it was easier to get on the pill than it was to talk to my partner about protection. Fear is a very powerful tool. It can freeze up your mind, your heart and your soul. This fear can also lead you down a very dangerous path where sometimes there is no looking back. I wish I had a dollar for every time in the past [three years] that I've said or thought, "If only I'd...."

I finished my bachelor degree at St. Edward's University in Austin, Texas and went to the American Academy of Music and Dramatic Arts in New York City for graduate studies with the hope of launching my Broadway career.

After losing my virginity at 21, with an old friend, I only had three other sexual partners before I met my husband, Al. In September of '92, I met Al on a nine-month national tour of Cinderella. I wasn't Cinderella and he wasn't the prince. I was one of the evil, not ugly, stepsisters. Al was the music director. It didn't take us long to realize that we were falling in love. As we continued to cross the country, month by month I began to get sick. By March '93, I was very sick and in early April, after much angst, I resigned from the tour one month before it ended and returned to my parents' home in Dallas.

I asked our family physician to run an HIV test. He laughed but he agreed to do it. The test came back positive, and within a few more days I learned that I had already progressed to AIDS. I was devastated. I had to call Al who was still on tour and tell him to get tested. He did and he also turned out to be HIV positive. Fortunately he had a high T-cell count and he still does today, so he is pretty healthy. By contacting our limited number of past sexual partners, we were able to determine that I most likely transmitted the virus to Al. And he is still in love with me, can you believe it?

Al finished the tour. In June '93 I moved to Denver, Al's hometown. We spent the summer getting engaged, getting settled and getting educated about HIV. In September we went public as an HIV positive heterosexual couple. I was the first Jewish woman in Colorado living with AIDS to go public. At that time I also set for myself some specific goals...that I would return to Texas and speak at my high school, synagogue and college.

One reason that I wanted to tell you my story was so that you would realize that AIDS is not just a "gay" disease. If it happened to me, it could happen to anyone. AIDS is an equal opportunity virus...men, women, children, gay, straight, Jew, Christian...this virus does not discriminate!

Failing health forced me to retire late in the fall of '93 from musical theater. Who would have ever thought that I would have to give up doing the thing that I loved the most at 25? I performed a little bit after that at different HIV functions, including the Colorado AIDS Walks and the first National Mothers March against AIDS held in Washington, D.C.

Al and I have spoken to thousands of people, young and old [many of them high school students]. We believe that we must educate people about all the facts and all their choices. We then trust that people will make choices that will reduce their risk of becoming infected.

I often say, "Having unprotected sex is like playing Russian roulette with your life and the life of your partner. Just don't load the gun. Misfortune randomly happens to people all the time, bad things that are unavoidable. However this virus is something you don't have to get!"

In August of '95, I developed acute pancreatitis. It was my first major illness because of AIDS. I was in the ICU in Denver General for 10 days on a respirator and in the hospital for several weeks after that. Over a period of months I have lost over 30 pounds. I weighed 94 pounds when I got sick. It is scary to be this thin.

It is now eight months later and I've gone through two surgical procedures, diabetic incidents and internal bleeding. I have managed to hang on and my spirit remains strong.

Although having HIV has brought many blessings into my life and made me appreciate every moment of living, it is still no fun to lie in bed, day after day, sometimes too weak to sit up, too nauseous to eat and too tired to do anything.

I still have dreams, though. My greatest hope now is that by hearing my story it will make you stop and think just a little more about your own lifestyle and protect yourself. As I said earlier, AIDS is no longer just that "gay disease" or an "IV drug abuser disease." There are no more high-risk groups, just high-risk behaviors.

Thank you for allowing me to share my story. Be safe, and follow your dreams for they are the hope for the future.

Best wishes,
Love,
Dee Dee

*Dee Dee was too ill by April 1996 to have delivered her message. The Denver Hebrew schools had requested a copy of her story to add to their curriculum and this is the statement Al prepared. After having done numerous presentations with Dee Dee, Al knew exactly what she would have said.

AFTERWORD

God answered so many of my prayers. Dee Dee gently and peacefully passed from this world. Today Al is doing well thanks to the advances in HIV treatments and a new love in his life. My husband was *not* infected from his needle stick. Our son and his wife gave birth to a beautiful healthy second son, Jackson Lynn Fields. (He is named for his Aunt Dee Dee, Diane Lynn Fields.)

My mother survived her accident. After five months in a nursing home, she regained almost all of her functions. She lived independently with Dee Dee's grandfather (who celebrated his 91st birthday in October 2000) until she succumbed to lung cancer in July 2000.

Dee Dee's dearest friend, Patrick, returned to school and earned his M.F.A. in directing. Howard and I were honored to attend his graduation from Texas Tech. He was an administrator of a major theater in a large city in the South, until he recently accepted a position to head the theater department for a magnet-type high school. We remain close friends thanks to e-mail.

The biggest aftershock happened six weeks following Dee Dee's death. Marie, her best friend, attempted suicide and was diagnosed with severe emotional problems. She had mental health problems that manifested in her belief that she had cancer and was dying. No, there never was any chemotherapy treatments, cancer or TB or the host of other maladies she claimed during and before Dee Dee's illness. Even though her condition originated long before Dee Dee's AIDS diagnosis, it escalated during that time. She received extensive treatment and therapy. Today she is married and makes her home on the East Coast. Although her feigned illnesses and other incidents brought stress into Dee Dee's life, more powerful was the strength and inspiration she offered Dee Dee throughout their friendship.

Al, after months and months of remorse, decided he could no longer go it alone. He met a lovely woman and remarried in October 1998. Howard and I attended the wedding. Al is currently the executive director of the People Living With AIDS (PWA) Coalition in Denver where he works with his wife. He has, for the most part, given up his theatrical/music career. Al's immune system began to show some signs of decline in January 1999. He started HAART (highly active antiretroviral therapy) and today, thanks to the new treatments, has an undetectable viral load.

Many events have occurred to honor Dee Dee's memory. Two weeks following her funeral in Dallas, a special celebration of her life was held on a Monday evening in a Denver theater, the night that theater is traditionally dark. Over 300 people attended. Her husband planned and directed a beautiful, moving tribute to her life.

In December 1997, when a new chapter of the NAMES Project was formed in Denver, we turned over a quilt panel that Al and I had designed to reflect Dee Dee's life. It was a collaborative work lovingly sewn by Al, Al's then fiancée, Shelley, Denise, Marie, Marie's mother and some other friends. The panel has a sun, clouds, and a music staff with a few notes from "Somewhere Over the Rainbow" and a rainbow on it. Her quilt is shiny, feminine, pink and very bright. We believe Dee Dee would have approved. Al sewed his wedding band into the third spoke of the sun. Whenever her panel goes "on tour," he is with her.

Thanks to a large contribution to Congregation Beth Torah from Dee Dee's grandparents, Howard and I purchased a torah and held a special dedication ceremony for it in January 2000. This Torah is about 100 years old, of Russian origin, lightweight and small. Dee Dee would have loved it and been pleased that it was earmarked for use by the children of Beth Torah.

In June of 1999, shortly after I began to write this book, I sent a letter to many people in Dee Dee's life. I asked them to share their favorite memories of Dee Dee. The responses to my letters were heartfelt. Many of the stories have been included in the body of this work.

Dee Dee's husband, Al, offered these reflections three years after her passing: "We met on a national tour of *Cinderella*. We fell quickly in love. In April 1993 she was diagnosed with HIV/AIDS and I tested positive afterwards. In one day our lives were dramatically and irreversibly changed. We walked wide-eyed and hand in hand into this world we call our HIV community. We were welcomed with open arms. Dee Dee's dream to go public five months later launched us into AIDS PR. We shattered the Neanderthal stereotypes the general public had about this 'gay' disease.

"I learned so much from Dee Dee: how to love, how to give, and what true commitment was about. Dee Dee was a person of incredible grace and compassion, love, integrity, courage and persistence.

"She was a petite woman with a voice as big as the Rockies. She had boundless energy and enthusiasm for life and for her work. She was inspirational, courageous and beloved by many. She changed my life and the life of many with her story. She was a blessing to this world and I am honored to have been able to share her life as her husband and caregiver. She was my princess and I her white knight and we lived our lives together with the knowledge that time was ours only for the moment and love was all!"

To our Dee Dee from Mommy and Daddy,

> You came into our lives and all-too-quickly went away.
>
> You moved our souls to dance.
>
> You awakened us to new understandings with the passing whisper of your wisdom.
>
> You made the sky more beautiful to gaze upon. After a rain, you always looked for the rainbow.
>
> You stayed in our lives for a while, left foot-prints on our hearts, and we will never, ever be the same.

"Mommy, you did it. You found the gift I left you—my story."

APPENDIX I

NATIONAL AIDS SERVICES
Resources and Publications

AIDS Educational Global Information
www.aegis.com

AIDS, Medicine & Miracles
www.csd.net/~amm
e-mail: amm@csd.net

AIDS Treatment News
800-873-2812
PO Box 411256
San Francisco, CA 94141
www.aidsnews@aidsnews.org

Being Alive
310-289-2551 621 San Vicente Blvd
West Hollywood, CA 90060
Fax: 310.289.9866
www.mbay.net/~bngalive/index.html

BETA: Bulletin of Experimental Treatments for AIDS
San Francisco AIDS Foundation
800-833-0159
www.sfaf.org/beta.html;
beta@thecity.sfsu.edu.

Center for Disease Control
www.cdcnac.org

CMV Hotline
800-838-9990

Critical Path AIDS Project
www.critpath.org/critpath.html

Cyber Beacon
www.beaconclinic.org

Gay Men's Health Crisis
www.gmhc.org

Health Communication Group
www.healthcg.com

HIV/AIDS Treatment Information Service
800-448-0440

Informacion Tratamiento SIDA
809-723-8582
HIV Newletter in Spanish
c/o Juan Perez Mendez
110 Calle Colomer #4D
San Juan, PR 00907

NATIONAL AIDS HOTLINE
800-342-2437

National AIDS Treatment Advocacy Project
www.natap.org

HOME HIV TEST (approved by the FDA)
Home Access: 800-448-8378
www.homeaccess.com

National Trials Information
800-874-2572

Notes from the Underground PWA Health Group
212-255-0520
150 W. 26th Street, Suite 201
New York, NY 10001

Positive Living, AIDS Project L.A
323-993-1362
Publications Program
1313 N. Vine St.
Los Angeles, CA 90028
www. Apla.org
e-mail: Pserchia@aol.com

Positively Aware
Test Positive Network
773-404-8726
1258 W. Belmont Ave.
Chicago, IL 60657-3292
Fax: 773-404-1040
www.tpan.com
e-mail: tpanct@aol.com

POZ Magazine
www.poz.com
e-mail: edit@poz.com

PROJECT INFORM
Hot Line: 800-822-7422
205 13th Street #2001
San Francisco, CA 94103
Phone: 415-558-8669
Fax: 415-558-0684
International: 415.558.9051

Resolute
303-329-9397
PWA Coalition Colorado
1290 Williams Street
Denver, CO 80302
PWACOLO@aol.com

Teen HIV Hotline
800-440-8336

University of California San Francisco AIDS Program
hivinsite.ucsf.edu

Women Alive
800-554-4876
www.thebody.com/wa/wapage

Women and AIDS
www.zumacafe.com/pocaf/women.html

WORLD
Women Organized Responding to Life-threatening Diseases
510-658-6930
PO Box 11535
Oakland, CA 94611

Women's Tx News
212-255-0520
c/o PWA Health Group
150 W. 26th Street
New York, NY 10001

APPENDIX II

GLOSSARY

Acute HIV Infection: The time following HIV infection (4 to 7 weeks) during which the body mounts an immune response to HIV virus. About 30% to 70% of people will experience flu-like symptoms (fever, fatigue, headache, swollen lymph glands and/or rash) during this time. Another name for this time is Primary Infection.

ADAP: AIDS Drug Assistance Program. These are state-based programs providing HIV medications and opportunistic infection treatments for little or no cost. These programs are funded in part by Title II of the Ryan White Care Act and each state determines eligibility criteria.

Antibodies: Proteins made by the immune system that identifies, marks, and destroys disease-causing organisms like bacteria and viruses.

Antiretrovirals: Medications that stop or slow the replication and activity of HIV.

CD4+ Cells: White blood cells that coordinate the immune response to fight bacterial and viral infections. In HIV the CD4+ is a marker used for measuring immune system health. Normal count is between 500 and 1500 per cubic milliliter of blood. HIV infection with a CD4+ count below 200 is considered an AIDS diagnosis.

Clinical Trial: An investigative study involving humans in order to determine if an experimental treatment is safe and effective, to uncover potential complications, and to discern what must be done on any new drug(s) before it is approved for widespread use.

ELISA Test: Enzyme-Linked Immunosorbent Assay. This is a common diagnostic test to detect the HIV antibodies in a blood or saliva sample. If two ELISA tests are positive for HIV antibodies and the more sensitive Western Blot test is positive, it will confirm the presence of HIV infection.

HAART: Highly Active Antiretroviral Therapy. Aggressive HIV treatment involving a combination of HIV drugs with the goal of stopping replication of the virus and lowering a person's viral load to undetectable levels. Sometimes referred to as "the cocktail."

HIV Disease: HIV infection, including initial infection, seroconversion, asymptomatic and symptomatic HIV infection and AIDS.

HIV-1: Human Immunodeficiency Virus Type 1. The retrovirus most commonly associated with HIV disease. It is currently the most common strain of HIV virus and accounts for the majority of global HIV infection.

HIV-2: Human Immunodeficiency Virus Type 2. Another strain of HIV virus considered less virulent and it is less widespread. HIV-2 is primarily found in West Africa and Southeast Asia.

Long-Term Nonprogressor: HIV positive people who are positive for at least 7 years, with stable CD4+ cell counts over 600 and no HIV-related opportunistic infections, despite never having used antiretroviral therapy.

Microbicide: Protective substance containing bacterial/viral-killing agents that can be applied to the vagina, rectum, mouth or other skin. If developed, these could be used to protect HIV and STD infection especially in situations where condoms won't or can't be used.

OI: Opportunistic Infection. This is an illness that occurs when the immune system is too weak to keep it in check. Examples of HIV-related OIs are PCP (Pneumocystis carinii pneumonia), Kaposi's sarcoma, shigellosis, toxoplasmosis and HPV (human papillomavirus)-related cervical cancer in women. HIV infection and having had one or more OIs and a CD-4 count less than 200 equals an AIDS diagnosis. In many cases, it is the opportunistic infections that cause death in AIDS patients.

Seroconversion: The development of a detectable amount of antibodies to a particular infectious agent. HIV seroconversion may take anywhere from a few weeks to six months depending on the individual. And there have been rare cases where this has occurred after six months.

Viral Load: Amount of measurable HIV found in blood or other body fluid sample.

Western Blot: This is a sensitive laboratory test that detects the presence of HIV bodies in a blood or saliva sample. This test is used as a final confirmation after a positive ELISA test. If both tests were reactive then a person would be considered positive for HIV infection.